The Plough and the Sword

THE PLOUGH AND THE SWORD

Labor, Land, and Property in Fascist Italy

By

CARL T. SCHMIDT
DEPARTMENT OF ECONOMICS, COLUMBIA UNIVERSITY

. . . O Blackshirts, O veterans, the arms of the Nation must be very strong. For the plough drives the furrow, but the sword defends it . . . Now you know why you heard the voice of the cannon thunder alongside mine.
—*Mussolini*

New York: Morningside Heights
COLUMBIA UNIVERSITY PRESS
1938

Published 1938

Printed in the United States of America

Preface

Fifteen years ago the Fascist party came to power in Italy. Since that day late in October 1922, when Benito Mussolini succeeded Luigi Facta as Prime Minister, Fascism has come to dominate the life of the Italian people. Similar methods of action and thought have risen to triumphant or potential domination elsewhere in the world. And people everywhere ask the meaning of Fascism.

The Italian Fascist leaders constantly speak of their concern for the welfare of the rural population. They declare that Fascism is "ruralizing" Italy, that it unceasingly champions the economic cause of the peasants and that it has given them, for the first time in history, a voice in the political life of the nation. Fascism, they say, is primarily a "rural phenomenon." Many commentators have accepted this claim and have done much to spread it in the world. Yet it is possible that Fascism-in-action is something very different. This, and the importance of the rural community—peasants and landed proprietors—in the life of Italy suggest the significance of a critical study of agriculture under Fascism.

The formal structure of the Corporative State and its alleged meaning for the Italian people have been frequently and exhaustively described. But the present study is concerned with the behavior of Fascism, with its bearing on work and life, on peasants and proprietors and their relations to bread and land. It deals with forms and professed objectives only as points of departure. Its purpose is to contribute toward an understanding of Fascism.

The study, of course, is limited by the quantity and quality of the data on which it is based. "Impartiality," in the sense of pretending not to have social values, has been impossible. Yet no available data, whether favorable or unfavorable to Fascist avowals, have been deliberately ignored or distorted. Moreover, the sources are predominantly Fascist—official reports, and speeches and writings of Fascist leaders and followers. The authorities do not provide all the information that one might desire—this has been especially true during the last two years. And such information as has been made available is biased by the spirit and purposes of the regime. The official bias, it seems safe to assume, is overwhelmingly in one direction and will almost never represent conditions as unfavorable to Fascist claims. Gibbon says that the Persians, in exaggerating the size of their population and resources, "seem to have indulged one of the meanest, though most common, articles of national vanity." Such bias, then, is by no means peculiar to a Fascist regime. But the student of Fascism labors under the special disadvantage of finding little truth other than the official truth. The semi-official truth is hidden—sometimes within the folds of the official truth, to be sure—and is not easy to discover.

I am deeply indebted to the Social Science Research Council, of New York City, which in 1935 granted me a research fellowship for study in Italy. I am also very grateful to the International Institute of Agriculture, in Rome, to members of its staff, to officials of the Italian government, and to others who facilitated my research. To those who have read the manuscript and have made valuable suggestions, I offer my sincere thanks.

Acknowledgment is made to the editors of the *Journal of Farm Economics*, the *Marxist Quarterly*, *Science and Society*, the *Living Age*, the *Manchester Guardian*, and the *Political*

Science Quarterly, for their kind permission to use materials that have appeared under my name in these journals. The quotation on the title-page is from a speech by Mussolini at Littoria, December 18, 1934; that opposite the first page is from Ignazio Silone, *Bread and Wine* (Harper and Brothers, 1937), and is reproduced by permission of the publishers.

CARL T. SCHMIDT

Columbia University
New York City
October 28, 1937

Contents

The Plough and the Sword

"The truth is officially as follows . . . Bolshevism reigned here, and religion, morality, and private property were being trampled under foot. Then came Etcetera Etcetera, and religion, morality, and private property were restored."

"We are now neither in the market place nor in the pulpit. . . . The official truth we know. But what is the semi-official truth?"

"The semi-official truth . . . is that what reigned here was ignorance and hunger. The poor people started organizing themselves into leagues. Then came Etcetera Etcetera, and destroyed the leagues, but not the hunger, which has increased since."

—Ignazio Silone

I: Rural Italy

When September comes to Fontamara,
the hard life that donkeys, men and women lead
becomes, if anything, harder still.

—IGNAZIO SILONE[1]

THE economic life of Italy is basically rural. Although urban industry has become increasingly important during the past generation, nearly half of the Italian people still gets its living directly from the soil. The rural population bulks large in every part of the country and is preponderant in most regions. Moreover, the processing and marketing of agricultural commodities are important functions of Italian industry and commerce.

Italy's peasants and farmers supply a major proportion of the country's food requirements, and contribute substantially to its exports. But the demands of a population that is strikingly large in terms of the available natural resources and current techniques make this a difficult task. It is achieved only by a heavy outlay of human effort. The unending, hard work of peasant men and women, cultivating every available plot of earth, even on steep hillsides, gives Italy its agricultural riches.

A large part of the country is mountainous and arid; only a relatively small area is naturally fertile and easily tilled. Nevertheless, more than two-thirds of the land is under cultivation or in pasture, and most of the remainder is used productively.

[1] *Mr. Aristotle* (Robert M. McBride and Company, New York, 1935). Reprinted by permission of the publishers.

Italy is often referred to as the "Garden of Europe," but it is a mistake to interpret this as meaning that the country is uniformly rich in agricultural production. A large area is occupied by rocky and unproductive mountains. Past generations are responsible for the destruction of the forests that clad these mountain sides, and this has resulted in unregulated water courses of a torrential character, with seasonal floods alternating with droughts. Much has been done in the past thirty years to reclaim marsh lands, but there still are large areas of swamps with the attendant evil of malaria. Few European countries have so large a proportion of their territory irredeemably unsuited to agriculture or reclaimable only at a heavy capital outlay. The agricultural wealth which Italy can claim is not so much due to the bounty of nature as to the diligence of her farmers. Even the rich plains of Lombardy are the creation of past generations, who drained, leveled, irrigated, and fertilized them. The bare mountain sides of Liguria have been terraced and the very soil brought to them on the backs of men and women. The swamps of Venetia, the Tuscan Maremma, the low-lying country at the mouth of the Po around Ravenna have been drained and reclaimed by the industry of the inhabitants.[2]

Italian agriculture is extremely varied as to crops, methods of cultivation, types of farm enterprise, and labor-employer relations. This reflects the diversity of the country in natural endowments and cultural patterns.

[2] Hobson, *The Agricultural Survey of Europe: Italy*, p. 9. See also Valenti, "Italian Agriculture in the Last Fifty Years"; Federzoni, *I problemi attuali dell'agricoltura italiana.*

The total area of Italy in 1929 was about 31,000,000 hectares. This consisted of 23,000,000 hectares in farm land, 5,500,000 in woods and forests, and 2,500,000 in roads, building sites, etc., and in waste land. Istituto Centrale di Statistica, *Annuario Statistico, 1936*, p. 43. According to the Ministry of Agriculture, 35.5 per cent of Italy's land area is "mountainous," 52.5 per cent "hilly," and only 12 per cent "plain." Much of the "woods and forest" area is covered by shrubs and widely scattered trees.

The physical contrast between North and South is the most obvious: Continental Europe ends in one, North Africa begins in the other. Within these extremes of generalization, several main regions, differing in surface structure and climate, are marked out by the Alpine wall, the long chain of the Apennines, and the sea.

Hemmed in by the escarpment of the Alps and the northern slopes of the Apennines lies the broad plain watered by the Po and its tributaries. Climatically—in the sharp contrast between summer and winter—this region is definitely continental. No part of Italy has hotter summers, but the winters are colder than those of Denmark. Periods of frost and snow are common. Rainfall is abundant throughout the year, reaching a maximum in spring and summer. The western portion is well drained, but toward the Adriatic are low-lying areas that require artificial drainage and dykes to prevent floods and swamps. Natural advantages and the patient efforts of generations of rural workers have made the Po basin one of the richest agricultural regions of Europe.

Beyond the Apennines the climate at the lower altitudes is essentially Mediterranean: winters are mild and rainy, summers dry and warm. Fertile coastal plains—those of Tuscany and Latium—are connected with each other by hilly regions sheltering small, rich valleys. Near the sea these plains tend to be swampy. Most of the central and southern region, however, is mountainous, dry, and barren. Toward the far south the mountains are increasingly rugged and bleak. They are broken by gulleys through which, in the rainy season, torrents race, sweeping the surface soil rapidly off the deforested slopes. Parts of the western littoral of the South are fertile, as, for example, the volcanic plain of Naples and the Calabrian shores, but everywhere in the interior uplands the country is arid and rocky. At the southeastern tip of the peninsula are the parched tablelands of Apulia.

Sicily is also a region of contrasts. The lower slopes of the mountains in the north and the west are fertile and favorable to intensive agriculture, but most of the remainder of the island is an arid plateau. The meager rainfall is concentrated in the autumn and winter. Summers are dry and scorched by the sirocco, blowing off the African deserts. Sardinia is a country of malarial lowlands and bare, dry mountains.

Such differences of altitude, soil, and climate allow the cultivation of a great variety of crops, ranging from rye, apples, and hemp to rice, oranges, and cotton. Nearly a third of the farm land is under cereals, of which wheat and corn are the most important. Wheat is produced everywhere, in mountains, hills, and plains. Corn is a leading crop in the moister lands of the North, and is also cultivated elsewhere. Rice is planted in the Po basin and along the river valleys of the east coast. Sugar beets and tobacco are becoming increasingly important, especially in the North. Root crops, vegetables, deciduous fruits, grapes, and flax are grown throughout the country. Silk cocoons, chestnuts, hemp, and flowers are regional specialties in North and Central Italy, and olives, almonds, and citrus fruits are largely produced in the South. The dairy and hog industries are important only in the North. Elsewhere cattle have more significance as work animals than as sources of milk or meat. Goats and sheep are to be found in every part of the country, and are particularly prominent in the South.[3]

[3] The farm land in 1929 was distributed as follows: about 12,700,000 hectares in sown crops (including fields on which trees were growing in association with sown crops), 2,300,000 in tree crops, 6,000,000 in artifi-

The methods and organization of farming are quite as varied. Extremes are represented by the highly commercialized and mechanized farms of the Lombard plain and the primitive village economy of the mountainous Abruzzi and Sardinia, where hoe and sickle are the chief tools, crop rotation is based on traditional formula, and threshing is done by the animals.

In the Alpine districts of Lombardy, Venetia, and Piedmont, stock breeding and forestry industries are pursued on lines not unlike those of Switzerland; in the irrigated valley of the Po the farming is that of the most progressive countries of Northern Europe; in the districts of Polesine and Ferrara in the Venetian provinces, where land reclamation and drainage projects have been developed extensively, farming is similar to that carried on in the rich pasture districts of Holland. The vineyards of Piedmont are comparable with those of France; those of Latium, Apulia, and Sicily with Spanish vineyards. The highly diversified farms of Tuscany, where wheat is grown between rows of vines festooned from branch to branch of willow trees which act as their props, with fruit trees scattered about the fields, and olive groves utilizing the otherwise barren hill-sides, are characteristically Italian. . . . The large wheat farms of the Apulian table-land with their industrialized agriculture, exhibit a form of farming similar to that prevailing in Eastern Europe.[4]

Cultivation throughout most of Italy is very intensive, not only where there is small peasant proprietorship and tenancy,

---

cial and natural pasture, and 2,000,000 uncultivated. The chief crop areas, in millions of hectares, were: cereals, 7.1; legumes, including beans and other pulses, 1.1; industrial crops, including sugar beets, hemp, flax, and tobacco, 0.2; potatoes, 0.4; vegetables, 0.2; forage, 8.9; vines, 3.9; olives, 2.0. Istituto Centrale di Statistica, *Annuario Statistico, 1936*, pp. 43-45. It is common to grow several crops at once on the same field, hence the total of individual crop areas is greater than the total farm area. For data on the live-stock population, see below, pp. 61-62.

[4] Hobson, *op. cit.*, p. 8.

but also on the big commercial farms of the North. On the other hand, the great estates of the Roman Campagna, Lucania, Calabria, and Sicily are generally utilized as sheep pasturage or wheat fields and represent an extensive fallow system of agriculture.

Small-scale peasant and share-tenant cultivation is important in the Po region, but the peculiar character of its agriculture is given by commercial farming. Most of the land belongs to urban proprietors who rarely cultivate it themselves, but instead rent it out under various systems. Particularly significant are the large cash-tenant farms producing mainly corn, rice, and dairy products. Irrigation—of great importance in this region—has had a concentrating effect on farm enterprise, inasmuch as the expensive works are most effectively undertaken on a large scale. The bigger farms are thoroughly industrialized and employ complex, mechanical techniques. Much of the intensive field work is done by laborers under yearly contracts, living on the land, receiving part of their wages in kind, and perhaps having small plots of land at their disposal. The large farms also employ many casual day laborers, who live in the villages and towns. In Central Italy[5] share-tenancy is a major basis of farm enterprise. Here the peasant population is more nearly like that of France and Western Germany than elsewhere in Italy. Most of the farms are small, produce a considerable variety of crops, and tend toward self-sufficiency.

Quite different is the agricultural constitution of the South, or *Mezzogiorno*,[6] where the feudal pattern has been maintained most consistently. The agriculture of the hilly and mountainous sections (particularly in Central and Western

[5] Economically, Central Italy comprises Tuscany, Umbria, and the Marches.

[6] The *Mezzogiorno*, in an economic sense, includes all of peninsular Italy south of Tuscany, Umbria, and the Marches, as well as Sicily and Sardinia.

Sicily, Calabria, Latium) is dominated by the large, technically primitive, extensively cultivated estates. The absentee owners of these *latifondi* rent their land to usurious middlemen who sublet it from year to year in small plots to the cultivating peasants. The *latifondist* economy is characterized as follows:

The drought is the cause of the extensive cultivation; this, together with the bad water supply, is a source of malaria which is a formidable obstacle to intensive cultivation, and to the regular upkeep of water courses. The want of roads is a factor determining the absence of villages and hence the concentration of the peasants in the country towns, but this concentration explains and apparently justifies the absence of roads. For improvements in cultivation roads would be necessary, but the cultivation as it is at present does not make the construction of roads an easy matter. The countryside is deserted because of malaria, and the malaria spreads as a result of this very desertion. The lonely state of the countryside and the difficulty of communications are factors making for crime, but this in its turn means that the country is more and more deserted. Absenteeism is a cause of the decay of the *feudi*, but this decay is a potent cause of absenteeism.[7]

Impoverished peasants with tiny holdings are to be found throughout the South, in mountains and plains. In the Neapolitan Campania, however, and in parts of Southern Apulia and the Golden Horn near Palermo there is a highly intensive, garden-like cultivation of small orchards, groves, and vegetable fields by a relatively prosperous landowning and tenant peasantry. Throughout the South the peasants on the whole live not in the fields, but in villages and towns.

A very large proportion of the Italian agricultural population consists of dependent workers: share-croppers, share-tenants, small-holders who must supplement the inadequate

[7] Lorenzoni, "Latifundia in Sicily and Their Possible Transformation."

production of their minute plots of land by working for others, and wage laborers. According to the occupational census of 1931, roughly 8,000,000 persons over the age of 10 are engaged in agriculture. Of this number, about 3,000,000 are classed as "operating owners," 900,000 as "cash-tenants," 1,700,000 as "share-tenants," 2,500,000 as "wage-workers," and 27,000 as "managers."[8] But these data give an erroneous impression of the economic status of the rural population.

It is impossible to draw lines realistically between wage-workers, share-tenants, and small proprietors. For one thing, most share-croppers and share-tenants must actually be considered agricultural workers who are paid a share of the crops rather than money wages for their labor. Furthermore, many of the "operating owners," because their land is too limited to support them adequately, must gain a substantial (sometimes a major) part of their living from wage labor. They might reasonably be listed as wageworkers.

A detailed analysis of the many complicated kinds of employer-labor relationships would be beyond the scope of this study. The more important general types of labor may, however, be noted. (1) *Garzoni*—resident farm servants, generally employed on medium-sized farms and engaged in miscellaneous work; they are usually hired under yearly contract and are paid largely in kind. (2) *Salariati*—workers under

[8] The total gainfully occupied population of ten and more years of age is 17,262,521; 8,083,332 are occupied in agriculture. The total population of the country in 1931 was 41,176,671, of which number nearly 48 per cent was comprised in families whose head was employed in agriculture. The rural population constitutes about 55 per cent of the total population in the South, as against 49 per cent in Central Italy and 41 per cent in the North. Istituto Centrale di Statistica, *Censimento generale della popolazione . . . 21 aprile 1931*, Vol. IV. Data for any of the last thirty or forty years would not give a substantially different picture of the economic structure of the rural population.

yearly contract, employed on medium-sized and large farms, frequently engaged in specialized types of work and paid in varying proportions of cash and of kind. (3) *Obbligati*—day laborers under contract to work for a specific employer whenever required, the employer being bound, in turn, to give them the first chance of work. In view of widespread unemployment, this arrangement is of advantage to the workers and therefore they are generally paid by the day or hour at a lower rate than are the casual workers. (4) *Avventizi* and *braccianti*—casual day laborers. This class comprises the majority of agricultural wageworkers. They are generally paid by the hour or day (sometimes on a piece-work basis), and take employment wherever they find it, often at great distances from their homes, and sometimes in non-agricultural activities.

Share-croppers and share-tenants (*coloni parziari*) also are engaged under a large variety of contracts. Disregarding the diversity of details, two main types may be distinguished. (1) *Compartecipanti* or share-croppers—laborers who work with their families, sometimes with their own tools, on particular plots of land assigned to them by an employer. Their compensation is not a fixed wage in cash or in kind but a predetermined share of the crop (usually one-fourth to one-half), the expenses of cultivation being divided in the same proportion with the employer. Their work is carried on under the direction of the employer and they are dependent on his orders with respect to selection of crops and methods of cultivation. Sometimes a whole group of workers and their families are assigned land for cultivation under a collective contract of *compartecipazione*. (2) *Mezzadri* or share-tenants—workers who, with their families, are entrusted by a landlord with the cultivation of a more or less self-contained small farm. Their remuneration is also a predetermined share of the crops (usually one-half) and sometimes also the full proceeds from various minor farm activities. Although they usually have somewhat more independence than the *compartecipanti*, they work essentially under the control of the landlord (to whom they frequently are indebted), and thus in effect constitute a type of laborer. The share contract often passes from father to sons, one of whom takes over the management of the tenant farm while the others remain as his helpers. Vestiges of feudal economic relations—such as the obligation of the tenant family to perform certain household work for the proprietor, to provide his table with eggs, milk, and butter, to obtain his consent to the marriage of the sons—have tended to disappear during the last generation. In practice, share-cropping and share-tenant contracts vary greatly in regard to such details as the amount of work done on the assigned land by the cropper or tenant, the extent of working capital contributed by the landowner, the period of the contract, the terms for division of the crops and of expenditures. Finally, it should be observed that cash tenants often replace wage labor, and live and work under virtually the same conditions as share-tenants and wageworkers.

Agricultural wage labor in one form or another is to be found in every part of Italy. It is most prominent on the commercialized farms of the Po valley and of the reclaimed regions near the mouths of the Po, and on the orchards and extensive wheat farms of Apulia and Sicily. Share-tenancy is also widely diffused, but has special prominence in North and Central Italy, particularly in Emilia, Tuscany, the Marches, and Umbria. Peasant owners of dwarf and small holdings are scattered throughout the country. But only in the mountains is there a genuine land-holding, albeit woefully poor, peasantry.

In the main, the cultivators of the soil are separated from its ownership. Large proprietorship contrasts with a minute fractioning of the land. The economically independent farm owners, including absentee proprietors, probably do not number more than half a million. The great majority of farmers cultivate exceedingly small areas. The agricultural census of 1930 puts the total number of farm enterprises in Italy at about 4,200,000. Of these 1,500,000 (35.7 per cent) are one hectare (2.47 acres) or less in size, and therefore ought to be classed as dwarf holdings rather than as farms; 2,300,000 (54.6 per cent) are more than one and less than ten hectares in area; roughly 400,000 (9.7 per cent) cover more than ten hectares. The 3,800,000 dwarf and small holdings comprise but 32.7 per cent of all the farm land in the country, whereas the 400,000 large farms control 67.3 per cent thereof. These figures evince the extreme concentration of land ownership in relatively few hands.[9]

The agricultural population of Italy, then, is overwhelmingly proletarian in economic status, if not in sentiment. Working on a materially ungenerous land, with effective control of the means of production vested in absentee owners, it gets a precarious living at high human cost. The struggle of the rural masses to conquer these limitations is of the essence of Italy's history in our times.

[9] Istituto Centrale di Statistica, *Censimento generale dell'agricoltura . . . Censimento delle aziende agricole*. For further data see below, p. 139.

II: A Struggle against Poverty

"And what about the hierarchy?" . . .
"At the head of it all is God, lord of heaven.
Then comes Prince Torlonia, lord of earth.
Then comes the armed guard of Prince Torlonia.
Then come the hounds of the armed guard of
Prince Torlonia.
Then nobody else.
And still nobody else.
And still again, nobody else.
Then come the farmers.
And that completes the list."

—IGNAZIO SILONE[1]

A GENERATION ago the great masses of Italian peasants and farm workers lived in extreme misery. Wages were very low, hours of work were long, and employment was uncertain.[2] Heartless exploitation by gang-labor contractors, farm managers, and landlords was widespread. The share-tenants, while somewhat more secure than wageworkers, generally received a poor share of the crops, and were bound to render a variety

[1] *Fontamara* (Random House, Inc., New York, 1934). Reprinted by permission of the publishers.

[2] Daily wages of men farm workers at the beginning of this century ranged from 0.80 lira to 1.30 lira; those of women were as low as 0.35 lira. A day laborer's family in North Italy could earn but 250-400 lire a year. (Before the War the lira was equivalent to approximately 19 United States cents.) Sometimes wages were not fixed in advance; after the work was done the employer paid his workers what he pleased. Frequently payment was in the form of meager foodstuffs and poor habitations. Hours of work were generally from dawn to dusk, that is, about sixteen hours per day during the active, summer months. Day laborers could not count on employment for more than five months in the year. See Marabini, *Proletariato agricolo e fascismo in Italia;* De Rocquigny, *Le Proletariat rural en Italie;* Audoly, *La Protection légale des travailleurs agricoles en Italie.*

of uncompensated, feudalistic services to the landlords. The poverty of the workers and peasants was reflected in their crowded villages of small, dark, insanitary hovels, contrasting acutely with the picturesque and romantic impressions they so frequently gave to sentimental travelers. Unhygienic living conditions made the rural population the easy prey of terrible diseases. Particularly in the North, pellagra was rampant among the peasants, owing to their monotonous maize diet. Malaria was a characteristically rural disease in vast regions of the country. Epidemics of cholera and typhoid fever were frequent. The mass of the Italian rural population—bowed under hours of daily drudgery, earning the scantiest living, illiterate, fantastically superstitious, unhealthy—lived in conditions for which a parallel could hardly be found elsewhere in the Western World.[3]

Existence of the government was made known in the villages by the *carabinieri*, judges, and tax collectors. But the peasants took little or no part in the political life of the country. The government of united Italy served primarily the ascendant industrialists and the aristocratic landowners, and their interests ran counter to those of the underlying rural population. The suffrage was extremely limited, for the illiterate majority of the population was excluded. Thus the peasantry could not make even the motions of choosing parliamentary representatives, but was merely the raw material for the policies of those controlling the government.

[3] Detailed descriptions of agricultural conditions in the generation before the World War are contained in the official reports: Jacini, *Atti della Giunta per la Inchiesta Agraria: Relazione finale*; Faina, *Inchiesta parlamentare sulle condizioni dei contadini nelle provincie meridionali e nella Sicilia*. The Jacini inquiry concluded that "the condition of the Italian farm workers could not have been more sad at any time since the period of the Roman Empire."

The welfare of the masses of the countryside demanded free trade: full opportunity to exchange their wines, olive oil, fruits, and vegetables for the cheaper manufactured goods of Northern and Western Europe. The goal of the ruling class, however, was to make Italy a Great Power. This implied help by the State in enlarging and reserving home markets for the products of the North Italian industrialists and in extending their fields of exploitation abroad. Among the means to such an end were, of course, the conventional ones: imposition of restrictive tariffs and the levying of heavy taxes for maintenance of the armed paraphernalia of a Great Power. One result was that the government in its commercial treaties could hardly obtain favors for Italian agriculture. Industrial protectionism was countered abroad by retaliatory duties leveled against Italian farm exports. To be sure, the wheat producers, suffering from the competition of the New World, were given tariff aid. But this could be of profit only to producers with marketable surpluses of wheat, that is, to the larger farmers and great landowners.[4] Moreover, a community of interests between landowners and industrialists was developing through personal and financial relationships—a powerful buttress for the program of industrial protection. The peasantry and rural workers bore the substantial burden by paying high prices for domestic manufactures and by losing potential foreign markets for their own products. And the heavy national and local taxes, levied on almost every conceivable object of production and consumption, largely benefited the ruling class of towns and country.

The squalor of the peasantry was known in responsible quarters, and agrarian reform was a perennial subject of debate in the national parliament. Yet the authority and wealth

[4] See below, pp. 65 ff.

of the State did little or nothing to better the life of the rural proletariat. Some good work was done in the organization of public hygiene services, but this was only a palliative. The government had no coördinated plan of attack on fundamental rural problems. There was no lack of suggestions by well-intentioned individuals, but the money for translating proposals into action was seldom made available.[5] All this is hardly surprising. And it is not astonishing that, when the government did act, the interests of the bigger landowners were paramount. Thus, the drainage projects in North Italy, upon which the commercialization of agriculture in the Po valley during the nineteenth century depended in great degree, were originally financed with private capital. But by the middle of the century the growing scale of reclamation called for more capital than the landowners were able to obtain privately. The government—sensitive to these requirements—was prompt with assistance, and its aid became increasingly generous as time passed.[6]

The hostility and indifference of the dominant class toward the welfare of the agricultural masses was especially marked in the South. Despite nominal attempts at agrarian reform, the old order of landownership remained substantially unchanged. Under the terms of legislation of the Napoleonic period and the Risorgimento, the ecclesiastical and secular feudal holdings were to have been liquidated. But the local administrators, influenced by the aristocracy, permitted many of the holdings to remain under the control of great landlords. Such land as peasants did acquire was in many instances soon lost to them because of their lack of capital and passed back to the old aristocracy or into the hands of urban pro-

[5] See Valenti, "L'Italia agricola dal 1861 al 1911"; Bourgin, "La Question agraire en Italie," pp. 305 ff.

[6] See below, pp. 74 ff.

prietors. Thus absentee owners continued to rule in the South and to hold the peasantry in economic and political subjection, in poverty and ignorance. The new national government allowed this situation to continue, receiving in turn electoral support from the landlords. The Southern peasants became the stepchildren of united Italy; they particularly had to pay for the government's protectionist and fiscal policies. Some politicians, certainly, thought of solving the *problema meridionale* by developing a landowning peasantry and a small-scale industrialism in the South. But such hopes could not be realized so long as taxes and tariffs weighed heavily on the South, nor so long as the landlords, living *in absentia*, invested their earnings in Northern industrial enterprises.[7]

THE RISE OF ORGANIZED LABOR

In these circumstances, the rural workers were thrown back upon their own resources for the improvement of their lot. For a generation before the World War the countryside was in an almost continuous ferment of mass labor organization and wholesale emigration to countries where the prospects of living were brighter.

Although labor organizations were illegal before 1900, attempts, frequently violent, were made everywhere to develop them. Intermittently during the last quarter of the nineteenth century the widespread and growing discontent of the proletariat flamed forth in uprisings. The activities of Bakunin, Costa, Malatesta, and other exponents of the First International contributed much to awaken a revolutionary consciousness in the working class. Mass revolts, generally spontaneous, sporadic, and blind, occurred year after year in various parts

[7] See Silone, *Der Fascismus*, pp. 17-20. See also Arias, *La questione meridionale*; Azimonti, *Il mezzogiorno agrario quale è*; Fortunato, *Il Mezzogiorno e lo Stato italiano*.

of the country. Most prominent were the revolutionary movements of the *fasci*[8] in Sicily during 1890-94, in which hundreds of thousands of agricultural workers took part. These early agitations ended in bloody suppression by the authorities. With the turn of the century, however, the method of bayonet and prison gave way to the more subtle Giolittian policy of parliamentary bargaining, meager concessions, and division of the forces of discontent.

Mass migration from the South to the Americas began in the 80s, and assumed enormous proportions during 1900-1914. The consequent reduction of the labor supply and the inflow of capital by means of remittances from, and the return of, relatively prosperous emigrants led to a considerable amelioration of rural life in the southern provinces.[9] On the whole, labor organization did not flourish there. The Socialists, in contrast with their success in the North, made little headway—partly, apparently, because of bad tactics, partly because of the absence of a middle class capable of providing leadership for the movement.

But in the North the labor movement, led from the first by Socialists, grew rapidly after 1900. Local village unions ("leagues of defense") spread throughout the Po basin, and soon amalgamated into provincial federations. In 1901 a national organization of rural workers—the Federazione Nazionale dei Lavoratori della Terra, popularly called Federterra—was founded. At the end of 1906, when it joined the General Confederation of Labor, it comprised about 280,000 members, concentrated in Emilia and Lombardy, with a strong nucleus in Apulia. From the first these Socialist leagues employed all the familiar weapons of aggressive unionism, espe-

[8] *Fascio* (plural, *fasci*) means "bundle," "bunch," "collection," and in a figurative sense, "association," "league."

[9] See Foerster, *The Italian Emigration of Our Times.*

cially the strike and the boycott, to force employers to accept collective labor contracts. Rural workers engaged in more than 600 strikes in 1901-2, and thereby won an annual increase in wage payments of 48,000,000 lire. In all, during 1900-1914 there were 3,005 agricultural strikes (mostly in the North), involving as many as 250,000 workers in a single year.[10] Political victories of the Socialists, too, particularly in the conquest of many communal governments, helped to advance the cause of rural labor.

Agricultural-workers' unions were also organized under Roman Catholic auspices, especially in Northeast and Central Italy, but were relatively unimportant until after the War. In 1914 the Catholic rural unions had a membership of about 63,000. They were most successful among the share-tenants and small proprietors, who were little touched by Socialist propaganda and were traditionally tied to the Church.

Receiving their chief conceptual impulse from the encyclical *Rerum novarum* of Leo XIII, the Catholics (or "whites") looked largely to coöperation, local autonomy, and a greater diffusion of peasant proprietorship to improve rural living conditions. The so-called "red unions" sought, in principle at least, the goal of socialized agriculture. But the compromising tactics of "reformism" and "revisionism" were prominent in the Socialist movement.[11]

At first the poorly organized employers scarcely resisted the aggressive tactics of the unions. Collective contracts led to higher wage rates, a shorter working day, and generally im-

[10] Ministero delle Finanze, *Documenti sulla condizione finanziaria ed economica dell'Italia;* Marabini, *Proletariato agricolo e fascismo in Italia,* pp. 27 ff. Forty per cent of the strikes in 1912 resulted in higher wages. See also Arcari, "Statistiche salariali," p. 121.

[11] For accounts of these early agricultural mass movements, see Vöchting, *Die Romagna;* De Rocquigny, *Le Proletariat rural en Italie: Ligues et grèves de paysans;* Sartorius von Waltershausen, *Die sizilianische Agrarverfassung und ihre Wandlungen, 1780-1912.*

proved conditions. With the continuance of labor agitation, however, employers began to organize for defense. By 1909 some 54 proprietors' associations had been formed to combat the workers' movement. They raised strike reserve funds, and made use of the blacklist and strikebreakers.[12] The employers diminished their demand for wageworkers by introducing machinery, by curtailing cultivation of crops that require much labor, and by developing share-cropping and tenancy contracts. This increased unemployment, which in turn led the organized workers to demand still higher wages. It also obliged the unions to develop methods of resisting labor displacement, as for example the establishment of coöperative farms that absorbed part of the surplus labor; attempts to limit use of machinery and to require farmers to employ only the machinery owned by workers' organizations; the imposition of a "tax in workers" (requiring employers to hire a minimum number of workers per unit of cultivated land). This, of course, was serious interference with the basis of the private-property system.[13] Furthermore, because of the employers' preference for nonunion workers and discrimination against members, the unions attempted to force the unorganized into their ranks. Among other things this move involved a struggle against practices that tend to "bind the worker to the land," such as wages paid in kind and *compartecipazione*. The unions also pressed—and with success—for the execution of public works in which large numbers of rural laborers could be employed.

At the same time share-tenants, by increasingly exchanging work with other tenants and thus reducing the need for hired labor, often found themselves in conflict with the wagework-

[12] Bourgin, "La Question agraire en Italie," p. 295.

[13] See Hobson, "The Landless Agricultural Laborer in Italy" and "The Collective Leasing and Farming of Land in Italy."

ers' unions. In their effort to reduce this practice, these unions brought the pressure of boycotts, fines, and sometimes even destruction of crops to bear against the tenant farmers. Such narrowly monopolistic practices drove many tenants and small peasants into the Catholic and other non-Socialist organizations and thus were a source of dissension within the ranks of the agricultural masses. But the tenants were at odds with proprietors, too, as regards the terms of share contracts.

Despite the growing resistance of employers and despite much unemployment, the living standards of the workers rose appreciably. Official statistics of money and real wages show large advances between 1905 and 1920. A national index of real daily wages of ordinary men workers (1913-14 = 100) stands at 93 in 1905; 104 in 1910; 129 in 1915; and 150 in 1920.[14] Another study indicates a rise of 33.5 per cent in average real wages of agricultural day laborers throughout the country between 1913-14 and 1919.[15] These advances were much more substantial in the North—the main locale of the union movement—than in the South. The agricultural working day at the beginning of this century generally was "from sunrise to sunset"; in 1919 the Federterra secured the eight-hour day for all agricultural workers. Many contracts specified eight hours as the maximum in all seasons. Paid holidays for workers also were frequently stipulated.

Another step in the direction of workers' control of land was taken in the development of farming coöperatives. The coöperative movement in North Italy was allied from the first with trade unions. Farming coöperatives, for instance, had their origin in the necessity of providing subsistence for

[14] See Istituto Centrale di Statistica, *I salari agricoli in Italia dal 1905 al 1933*. See also p. 114 below.

[15] Confederazione Nazionale dei Sindacati Fascisti dell'Agricoltura, *I salari nell'agricoltura tratti dai contratti di lavoro dal 1913 al 1931*.

unemployed members of farm-workers' unions. As early as 1883 a group of Ravennese day laborers was organized to drain lands near the mouth of the Tiber and then to cultivate collectively the reclaimed area. By 1906 more than 50 collective farms were operating in the Po valley; the total number in Italy had grown by 1913 to 194. They proved to be a useful weapon in the struggle for better working conditions, not only by providing employment in slack periods, but also by securing revenues that could be used in financing strikes and in enabling workers to hold out in the face of employer resistance. Contrasting with these Socialist-inspired farm coöperatives, collectively managed and cultivated, were the coöperative land-leasing societies of Sicily, which rented large tracts of land from *latifondisti* and divided them into small plots for independent cultivation by the members. This last was a type of coöperation favored by the Catholics.

Coöperation in the processing of farm commodities, especially wine and dairy products, in purchasing industrial goods, and in obtaining credit was also growing in the pre-War period. Its greatest advances were made in the North. Many of the societies came under the influence of various political movements, Socialist, Catholic, and others, and were used to help recruit their popular followings. These forms of coöperation served the needs of peasant proprietors and tenants in greater degree than those of wageworkers.

Industrialization; a general rise in the technical efficiency of agriculture; and, more important, emigration—all had a part in raising the tenor of rural life.[16] Yet it is certain that the great advance realized by the agricultural workers is attributable in larger degree to the activities of the unions. They were

[16] For evidence of high positive correlation between emigration and wage rises, see Sartorius von Waltershausen, *Die sizilianische Agrarverfassung und ihre Wandlungen*, p. 285.

effective, not only in raising wages and in reducing the agricultural working day, but also in providing better distribution of employment among the available labor supply. This was accomplished by setting up employment bureaus and by the establishment of the "tax in workers." The organized workers' movement, particularly as represented by the Socialists in the national parliament (the franchise was greatly extended in 1912), created much of the impetus behind the adoption of social legislation. Continual pressure led to the passage of laws providing for hygienic control of certain types of work,[17] compulsory and free distribution of quinine in malarial regions,[18] the recognition of collective labor contracts, compulsory accident, old age, invalidity, and unemployment insurance, and government-supported employment agencies.[19] Moreover, the Socialist movement made increasing numbers of middle-class Italians aware of the miserable economic and cultural conditions of the rural population; it helped to shake the peasantry out of its passivity and torpor; it did much to change the relationships between landlord and peasant "from that of master and servant to that of man and man."[20]

Nevertheless, the income of the rural population on the eve of the World War was still very low. The total annual net income of agriculture just before the War is estimated to have been 6,600,000,000 lire (as against a national income of about 19,000,000,000). Of this total, 3,650,000,000 was capital income, flowing mainly to landlords and large, capitalistic

[17] For instance, that of the notoriously exploited rice-field workers.

[18] The ravages of malaria and pellagra were greatly reduced during 1900-1915.

[19] See Audoly, *La Protection légale des travailleurs agricoles en Italie*; International Labour Office, "Collective Agreements in Italian Agriculture."

[20] Serpieri, *La politica agraria in Italia*, p. 31. It may be noted that collective bargaining in agriculture was established in Italy well before it had any significance elsewhere in Europe.

tenants. The remainder, 2,950,000,000, constituted labor remuneration and was almost the sole income of the peasantry, small tenants, and farm wageworkers.[21] Thus the cultivating masses, more than half of the country's population, received less than a fifth of the national income. And the rural workers' movement had produced no important change in the control of agricultural enterprise. The great bulk of Italian landed property was still in the hands of the aristocracy and the wealthy middle class. It was said, "In Italy there are 30 million people ruled by 30 men in the interests of 300,000 families." According to an estimate made in 1912, there were then nearly 5,000,000 "landowners" in Italy, but 70 per cent of the land belonged to only a quarter of a million proprietors. More than 3,000,000 "landowners" possessed less than one hectare each.[22] In many instances these peasant holdings consisted of only a single tree or row of vines—"not even land enough to be buried in!" as the peasants insisted.

THE WAR AND ITS AFTERMATH

The decade before the World War witnessed an acceleration in the monopolistic development of Italian capitalism. Increasingly, the economic power of the iron and steel, machinery, textile, munitions, and shipbuilding industrialists of the North was extended and its control concentrated through the medium of the big banks. Their concurrent political power was reflected in expanded armaments, the Tripolitan expedition, and Italian intervention in the World War. Dur-

[21] Serpieri, *La guerra e le classi rurali italiane*, pp. 16-19; McGuire, *Italy's International Economic Position*, p. 447.

[22] Mortara, *Doveri sociali della proprietà fondiaria*. The concentration of landownership was especially marked in the South. For example, in 1907 nearly one-third of the total area of Sicily (whose population then was 3,500,000) was the property of 787 individuals, and nearly one-sixth of the island belonged to only 173 individuals. See Lorenzoni, "Latifundia in Sicily," p. 327.

ing the War these tendencies progressed even more rapidly. It was a period of high profits for the great industrialists and financiers, of further consolidation of their economic and political controls. The commercialization of agriculture in the North also continued; more emphasis was put on machine methods of production and on industrial crops.

The World War brought heavy sacrifices to the rural masses, at home as well as at the front.[23] On the whole, the poorer peasants, in consequence of the loss of man power and the governmental policies of price control and requisitions, paid dearly for the maintenance of the war machine. As the slaughter dragged on, month after month, with victory uncertain, old animosities grew. A bitter resentment spread among the *contadini* against townsfolk, landlords, and industrialists—whom they blamed for having brought Italy into the conflict for selfish purposes; they came to believe that they were being exposed to death and misery for the profit of others. Moreover, the Russian Revolution was an inspiration and a promise to many rural workers. All this immensely whetted the old land hunger of the peasants. At the War's end they must be compensated for their losses by posession of the land.

The leaders of the unions and left-wing political parties encouraged this ambition.[24] And the politicians in power, hard put to hold the loyalty of the war-weary peasant soldiers, especially after the defeat at Caporetto, found it expedient to join in the cry: "The land to the peasants!" Their promises were generous but vague: once victory was won, the great

[23] See Serpieri, *La guerra*, pp. 41 ff., for evidence of the disproportionately great losses of the peasantry during the War.

[24] The Socialist General Confederation of Labor shortly after the Armistice included in its program a demand for socialization of the soil and cultivation by coöperatives and collective farms.

estates would be divided among the landless rural workers, and profit-sharing and factory control would be introduced for the benefit of industrial workers. Prime Minister Salandra declared in a speech:

> After the victorious end of the War, Italy will perform a great deed of social justice. Italy will give land and everything that goes with it to the peasants, so that every hero who has fought bravely in the trenches can become economically independent. That will be the Fatherland's reward to its brave sons.

This statement was printed and distributed widely at the front.[25]

Although the politicians' promises were hollow, the slogan "The land to the peasants!" did not remain altogether empty. During the War and the immediate post-War years there actually was a pronounced growth of peasant proprietorship. Certain more fortunate peasant cultivators profited from the rising prices of foodstuffs accompanying currency inflation. With their savings and borrowed funds they bought small patches of land from the wealthy proprietors. Many big landowners, disturbed by the growing disorders in the countryside, the talk of expropriation, and the increasing demands of farm labor, were less reluctant to part with their land than formerly. In this manner some 700,000 to 800,000 hectares passed into the hands of about a million small peasant families. However, this transfer of property did not produce a substantial change in the status of the peasant population; it represented, not a significant increase of autonomous family farms, but largely a rise in the number of dwarf holdings.[26]

[25] See Silone, *Der Fascismus*, p. 101.

[26] See Serpieri, *La guerra*, pp. 472-96, and the regional studies of tendencies in small proprietorship in the post-War period, *Inchiesta sulla piccola proprietà coltivatrice formatasi nel dopoguerra*, published by the Istituto Nazionale di Economia Agraria.

At the same time, a very considerable amount of land was also acquired by urban traders, war profiteers, and speculators, attracted by the possibility of gain in the rising values of inflation.[27] Thus a new and significant group of landowners emerged.

With the end of the War came difficulties in readjustment of the economy to a peacetime basis. One of the most serious of these was large unemployment among agricultural workers. Many farm employers, especially in the North, had been obliged during the War to carry on with little labor and so had come increasingly to use machinery. This led to resistance toward the employment of demobilized soldiers. The maintenance of urban industrial profits, too, called for lower labor costs.

All of these factors intensified the mass movement against the old order and, indeed, spread among the ranks of the working class a belief in the necessity of social revolution. In 1919-20 this revolutionary will among the workers expressed itself in an insurgent attack on private-property rights, in a great wave of agricultural and industrial strikes, and in the seizure of *latifondists'* land by peasants.

Both Socialist and Catholic rural movements reached their high points at this time. In 1920, when at their maximum strength, the Socialist unions had a membership of 889,000 farm wage workers and about 250,000 tenants, and the Catholic unions of workers, tenants, and small proprietors comprised 945,000 members.[28] The left-wing organizations used their

[27] Tassinari (in *Saggio intorno alla distribuzione del reddito nell'agricoltura italiana*) estimates the rise in farm land values between 1913-14 and 1921-22 as follows: Sicilian *latifondi*, 212 per cent; citrus groves, 283 per cent; irrigated land in Lombardy-Piedmont, 175 per cent; mixed crop land in Central Italy, 300 per cent.

[28] Confederazione Nazionale dei Sindacati Fascista dell'Agricoltura, *L'organizzazione sindacale agricola del fascismo*, p. 54; Marabini, *Proletariato agricolo*, p. 33.

mass pressure, in strikes on an unprecedented scale, to bring about further improvements in working conditions. In 1919-20 more than a million and a half agricultural laborers and tenants took part in 397 strikes, most of them ending in victory for the workers. (This fact also indicates the strength of the unions, especially the Socialist.)[29]

In consequence, wage rates were pushed up, the working day shortened, restrictions placed on the use of machinery, and employers subjected to further controls with respect to the placement of workers. Share-tenants—also through organized pressure[30]—forced landlords to grant them better terms. New contracts, many of them collective, gave the tenants a greater share of the crops, more secure tenure of the land, and a measure of control over the farm enterprises; they abolished lingering vestiges of feudal obligations to the landlords.[31] Under pressure of the left-wing political groups, the government took steps to curb rising land rents and to prevent landlords from evicting tenants, even at the expiration of their contracts.

The land-holding and land-cultivating coöperatives, too, were extended. They received encouragement from the gov-

[29] Serpieri, *La guerra*, pp. 274 ff. The "red" unions called 226 strikes, involving 1,170,000 workers, and the "whites" were responsible for 86, with 202,000 participants. The chief grounds were dissatisfaction with wage rates, working hours, and division of crops between landlords and tenants. According to Serpieri, 81 per cent of the strikes in 1919 and 85 per cent in 1920 resulted in complete or substantial concession of the workers' demands. The average duration in 1919 was 6.8 days; in 1920, 13.5 days.

[30] Share-tenants constituted 22 per cent of the total number of agricultural strikers in 1919, and 40 per cent in 1920. Serpieri, *La guerra*, p. 275.

[31] For data on wage developments, see below, pp. 111 ff. For details of the collective share-tenancy contracts of the post-War period, see Ministero per il Lavoro, *I concordati collettivi di lavoro stipulati dalla Federazione Nazionale dei Lavoratori della Terra*, pp. 85-105. See also Costanzo, "Share-Tenancy in Italy"; International Labour Office, "Collective Labour Agreements in Italian Agriculture."

ernment, which undertook to supply them with cheap credit through the agency of a bank for coöperatives and to lease them public lands on favorable terms. At the end of 1921 there were more than three hundred such societies, farming at least 150,000 hectares.[32] Special attention was given to peasants who were war veterans. The *Opera Nazionale Combattenti* (National Society of War Veterans)—organized in January 1919—was legally authorized to acquire land by donation and purchase, and, if capable of reclamation, by expropriation. Such land was to be leased or sold on easy terms to ex-soldiers. By the end of 1921 the *Opera* held approximately 50,000 hectares.[33]

In Central and Southern Italy—particularly in Latium, Apulia, Calabria, and Sicily—peasant leagues and coöperatives during 1919-20 took to direct action by invading large estates and putting the land under cultivation for their own purposes. Estimates of the total area thus occupied vary from 40,000 to 200,000 hectares.[34] According to Carleton Beals,

> groups moved *en masse* from the villages and squatted on sections previously marked out. Socialists went with their red flags; Catholics, often led by priests, went with their white banners; ex-soldiers, sometimes led by their former officers, went with the tricolor or black flags. The first group went to establish coöperative colonies; the two latter to establish peasant-proprietors.[35]

The ruling class and its governmental representatives was at first hesitant, even passive, before the threatening rural

[32] Ruini, "The Co-operative Movement in Italy," p. 27; Hobson, "The Collective Leasing and Farming of Land in Italy."

[33] Ruini, *op. cit.*

[34] In the summer of 1919 land-seizures occurred in 100 of the 128 communes of Latium. In the following year many of the *latifondi* of Sicily were occupied. See Ciasca, *Il problema della terra.*

[35] Beals, "Absenteeism, Kissed and Crowned."

and urban masses. Employers felt themselves obliged to accept the terms of collective contracts drawn up by the labor organizations. The land-seizures, of course, alarmed the governmental and landlord circles, but little or no resistance was offered. Indeed, the government through a series of decrees gave them a measure of legal recognition, at the same time attempting to head off further summary expropriation. The Visocchi decree (September 2, 1919) authorized provincial prefects to requisition "uncultivated or insufficiently cultivated" land and to cede it for four years to "responsible" coöperatives. At the end of the four-year period the final disposition of the land was to be determined by provincial commissions under a stipulated procedure. If the land was permanently transferred to a coöperative, indemnities to the former proprietors were to be fixed by arbitration committees.[36] This decree granted little, but many peasants interpreted it as merely the first step in a general expropriation program.

Politically, the radical and pseudo-radical parties made rapid advances. Their representation in parliament was much increased. In the national election of November 1919, a third of the votes were cast for Socialist candidates, and a fifth for candidates of the Catholic Populist Party, founded only ten months previously. Campaigning with definitely revolutionary language, the Socialists won 40 to 60 per cent of the

[36] A subsequent decree (the Falcioni decree of April 22, 1920) added further qualifications. The coöperatives must have financial and technical "competence"; if a coöperative failed to cultivate the land or pay for its use, the grant was to be rescinded; further arbitrary invasions were to be treated as acts of usurpation, punishable by fines and imprisonment. It is estimated that about 27,000 hectares belonging to 191 proprietors were requisitioned and ceded to 101 peasant coöperatives in the period September 1919-April 1920. See Rocca, "L'occupazione delle terre 'incolte'"; Serpieri, *La guerra*, pp. 283, 340 ff.

electors in Emilia, Piedmont, Umbria, Lombardy, and Tuscany. Also, many towns and districts in the North were governed by Socialists. In 1920, a quarter of all the communes and provinces in the country were under their control. Political victories were reflected in legislative action. A series of laws providing for the extension of social insurance and for government aid to the workers' coöperative movement was enacted. Politicians vied with one another in drawing up projects for division of the great estates among peasants. Opinion varied as to final disposal of the land—whether it ought to be parceled out among peasants for individual farming or ceded to coöperatives for collective cultivation—but there was an increasing conviction that large landed proprietorship must disappear.[37]

The agricultural labor struggle was, thus, but part of a revolutionary movement throughout the country. Everywhere the old dominant class of factory owners, landlords, tradesmen, and government officials was in retreat before the agricultural and industrial workers. When finally, in August-September 1920, half a million striking workers occupied factories all over the North, raised red flags, and proceeded to operate the plants, Italy appeared to be on the verge of social revolution.

[37] On these post-War developments in agriculture see: Serpieri, *La guerra;* Serpieri, *Studi sui contratti agrari;* Vöchting, *Die Romagna;* Silone, *Der Fascismus;* Marabini, *Proletariato agricolo.*

III: Counterrevolution

Only with Fascism have the peasants come into their full rights.

—MUSSOLINI[1]

YET revolution did not come. The leadership of the proletarian movement was divided, hesitant, and in part essentially conservative. That the leaders of the Catholic Populists were antirevolutionary goes without saying. Although their political appeal was patterned after that of the Socialists, their practical effect was to break the unity of the working-class movement and to reinforce the existing order. Many Socialists, however, also found themselves unable to accept a social overturn. Had the left-wing leaders been ready to seize political power in the autumn of 1920, the half-million workers occupying the factories and the hundreds of thousands of other organized workers might have insured victory. But the dominant group in the Socialist movement was not ready, and the Communists were unwilling to take the responsibility of leadership. The Socialist chiefs temporized in the face of the very opportunity for which they claimed to have been working so long. When they accepted as the solution of the "stay-in" crisis the compromise proposed by the government and secured, in exchange for evacuation of the factories, an empty promise to initiate workers' participation in industrial control, their movement had failed. It failed, many observers believed, because the "socialists" lacked the will to victory, and not because anyone else stood in its way.

[1] Serpieri and Mazzocchi-Alemanni, *Lo stato fascista e i rurali.*

The striking workers went back to their old jobs, disillusioned with their leadership.[2]

As the revolutionary wave ebbed, conservative elements in towns and country struck back at the Socialist organizations. They found a ready weapon for this purpose in the Fascist Party.

THE RISE OF FASCISM

In their early years the Fascists had attempted to rival the Socialists and Populists in demagogic demands for social reconstruction. Thus, Mussolini wrote in 1919:

> We are taking action not against the working class, but for it. We have so little concern for the bourgeoisie that we have put at the head of our program a demand for expropriation of large private fortunes, for confiscation of the war-time super-profits, for heavy taxation of capital. We will accept no kind of dictatorship.[3]

He applauded workers' violence against extortionate tradesmen, even supported occupation of the factories and the land-seizures. But the Fascists had at first little success in attracting any significant following. The earliest *fasci di combattimento* were composed of former revolutionaries who had been disowned by the working class parties; of disgruntled adventurers whose careers of violence had been cut short with demobilization of the army; of leaders of anti-Bolshevist leagues. In this period the outstanding characteristic of the *fascisti* was an extreme, violently nationalistic patriotism.

[2] The Socialist Party began to divide against itself. The Communist wing broke away in January 1921, to form a new party. In the national elections of May 1921, the number of Socialist deputies fell from 156 to 138 (including 16 Communists). Conflict continued within the Socialist ranks. Finally, in early October 1922, the "reformists" were expelled from the Party, which now sought readmission to the Communist International. But before the month ended the Fascists were in power!

[3] *Popolo d'Italia*, July 23, 1919.

However, as the revolutionary movement collapsed, the dominant class became aware of the value of hypernationalistic appeals reinforced by terrorism—the essence of Fascist demagogy. The industrialists and the big landowners, still sensing the danger of the labor organizations, called on the Fascists to crush them completely.[4] Moreover, enriched peasants, middle-class landowners, and small enterprisers—all the rural bourgeoisie who feared the threats of Socialism—streamed into the ranks of Fascism. The membership of the Party grew rapidly, rising during 1920 from 17,000 to about 100,000, and reaching 320,000 in the autumn of 1921, 477,000 in the summer of 1922.[5] Among the most ardent recruits were those who had won riches during the War, had increased their possessions of land, and were determined to hold their social position against the attacks of workers' unions, coöperatives, and Socialist-dominated communal governments. The peasants who had climbed into the middle ranks of landowners, tenants who hated the monopolistic practices of the unions, attorneys and merchants who had speculated in land during the inflation period, shopkeepers and traders whose business had been reduced by the Socialist

[4] The attitude of landed proprietorship was expressed in a speech at the first national convention of large landowners, held in Bologna, February 1921: "We are ready to defend our rights . . . not only to save ourselves, but also in order to defend civilization and progress. . . . We do not wish to strangle anyone, neither do we wish to be strangled, for we know that we are defending sacred personal rights and class rights." Quoted by Silone, *Der Fascismus*, p. 108.

[5] The occupational composition of the Party at the end of 1921 (as given in Por, *Fascism*, p. 121) is estimated to have been roughly as follows: agricultural workers, 20 per cent; commercial and industrial employees, 16 per cent; landlords, small farmers, and tenants, 16 per cent; students and teachers, 18 per cent; merchants and manufacturers, 15 per cent; professional men, 9 per cent; government employees, 6 per cent. But, of the total membership in mid-1922, nearly 60 per cent was said to consist of peasants and farm workers. See Mannhardt, *Der Fascismus*, pp. 186 ff.; Silone, *Der Fascismus*, p. 79.

coöperatives—all were quite as passionate defenders of the rights of property as were the great landowners. Thus in the countryside the *fasci* became weapons of landed and commercial proprietorship, united against the rural proletariat.

Supported by the money of big industrialists and landlords, tolerated and often actively helped by government officials, army officers, police, and judges, recruiting their mass following from the petty bourgeoisie of towns and country and also from the working class, the Fascists in 1921-25 waged an increasingly successful war against the old labor organizations. In the agricultural regions of North and Central Italy the punitive *fasci*, well supplied with man power and military resources, operated under the direct orders of the big landowners. Their offensive began with the destruction of the "Bolshevik" peasant and farm labor unions, then passed on to the smashing of the Republican and Catholic rural organizations. Socialists were ousted from local government posts; members of the unions and of peasant leagues were persecuted; union headquarters, newspapers, and coöperatives were demolished. It is estimated that in the first half of 1921 alone the Fascists destroyed 59 labor offices, 85 coöperatives, 43 rural workers' unions, 10 presses and 6 daily newspapers; they killed 202 workers, and wounded 1,144. The police arrested 2,240 anti-Fascist workers, and only 162 Fascists.[6] Ignazio Silone outlines the methods of the Fascist "expeditions" in the country. (1) The landlords of a district dominated or disturbed by "reds" call on the headquarters of the *fascio* in the nearest town for aid. (2) The *fascio* fixes a date for the expedition, prepares its weapons and vehicles, and presents its expense account to the landowners. (3) The police

[6] Silone, *Der Fascismus*, p. 110; Dutt, *Fascism and Social Revolution*, p. 124.

of the district, informed by the Fascists and the landowners, go to the "red" village or town in order "to prevent trouble"; that is, they search the houses of the union members, confiscate their weapons, arrest the bolder and more defiant workers, and assure the people that they need not fear the Fascist assault. (4) At night the *fascisti* come, escorted by the police, and get on with their work of demolishing union headquarters and coöperative shops, attacking leading members of the workers' organization, and the like.[7]

Thus the power of the left-wing movement was broken. More eloquent than the details of Fascist pillage and persecution are data on membership of the unions and on the number of strikes during this period. The membership of Federterra is said to have fallen from 889,000 in 1920 to 294,000 at the end of 1921—a loss of nearly 600,000—and it had shrunk to only 15,000 in 1924. The size of the Catholic unions also declined drastically.[8] Of the 8,000 coöperative societies affiliated in 1922 with the Socialist coöperative federation, only 2,000 remained in August, 1923.[9] The effectiveness of the Fascist counteroffensive is also reflected in the declining number of agricultural strikes in 1921-23, and in their unfavorable outcome for the workers. In 1921 there were 80 rural strikes, with 79,298 participants; in 1922, 23 strikes with 25,146 participants; in 1923, only one strike with 110 participants. In 1921, 40 per cent of the strikes resulted unfavorably for the strikers; in 1922, 48 per cent; and in 1923, 100 per cent![10]

[7] Silone, *Der Fascismus,* p. 111.

[8] Confederazione Nazionale dei Sindacati Fascista dell'Agricoltura, *I salari nell'agricoltura tratti dai contratti di lavoro dal 1913 al 1931,* p. 59; Serpieri, *La guerra,* p. 260-62.

[9] Lloyd, *The Co-operative Movement in Italy,* p. 108.

[10] Serpieri, *La guerra,* pp. 267, 279. For details of the Fascist reign of terror, see Salvemini, *The Fascist Dictatorship in Italy;* Silone, *Der Fas-*

In the towns the character and results of Fascism's attack on organized labor was much the same as in the country. The workers resisted, but their leadership was divided and indecisive. Consequently, their defensive strikes were desultory and weak. The Socialist leaders were unwilling to use any but legal weapons against the Fascists. The defeatism of the Socialists was expressed in the words: "Fascism cannot be conquered by armed, direct action, but only by legal means."[11] Repeatedly the union officials sought to obtain from the government promises of protection against the Fascist onslaughts. Such promises were given, but the authorities continually helped the Fascists, either by giving them legal and military assistance or by remaining benevolently neutral. Protest strikes and parliamentary speeches were no match for the guns of Fascists backed by the arms of the State.

Thus Fascism alone did not defeat the labor movement. Defeat was also the result of organized labor's internal weaknesses. But Fascism was the chief instrument of counterrevolution, wielded ostensibly in the interest of the petty bourgeoisie, actually in that of the big landowners, industrialists, and financiers. Its mission was violently to rebuild the superstructure of the existing State, in order to maintain and strengthen the State's social foundations.

Viewed historically, the "March on Rome" in October 1922, was but a step, and not a decisive one, in the development of the Fascist politico-economic system. Mussolini's accession to the premiership was followed by a period of "parliamentary" rule, coalition with non-Fascist political factions,

---

cismus; Nicoletti, *Le Fascisme contre le paysan.* For a Fascist version, see Volpe, "Fascismo: Storia," *Enciclopedia Italiana,* Vol. XIV, pp. 851-78.

[11] *Battaglie Sindacale* (organ of the General Confederation of Labor), January 29, 1931, quoted by Silone, *Der Fascismus,* p. 131.

and pursuit of an avowedly *laissez-faire* economic policy. It was not until the sweeping aside, in 1925-26, of the entire façade of democracy and libertarianism, and the establishment of the police dictatorship, that the political aspects of Fascism's mission were completed. Once firm control of the governmental machinery had been established, it was possible to give absolute predominance to the Fascist conception of employer-labor relations. An agreement with employers followed by legal measures finally destroyed all but the Fascist unions. This process was crowned by the syndical laws of 1926 and the "Charter of Labor" of 1927, which presumably lays down governing principles for relationships between capital and labor. The era of Fascist "class collaboration" began.

Through the period of monetary crisis and subsequent depression the processes of capitalist concentration and extension of power—both in urban industry and in agriculture—have continued, with organized working-class resistance eliminated and with full support by the State machinery.[12] The dominance of finance capitalism and absentee ownership, paying tribute to its praetorian guard of Fascism—such is the reality of the Corporate State. This reality is cloaked by the Fascist rationale of Corporativism as the alternative to capitalism and socialism, by its deification of the Leader, rituals of hypernationalism, and mysticism of the "elite." But the hollowness of Fascism's formal ideology is revealed by Mussolini's discovery in August 1921, that "if Fascism does not wish to die

[12] In 1929, the directors of the four leading banks (the Banca Commerciale, Credito Italiano, Banca Italiana di Credito, and the Banco di Roma) held 149 directorships in other banks, and 1,510 directorships in 839 industrial corporations with a total capital of 25,400,000,000 lire. These corporations comprised two-thirds of all the capital of Italian stock companies. For data on the concentration and centralization of capital in Italy during recent years, see Vandelli, "La marcia della concentrazione industriale"; Agreste, "Il capitale finanziario."

or, worse still, to commit suicide, it must now provide itself with a doctrine. . . . I do wish that during the two months which are still to elapse before our National Assembly meets, the philosophy of Fascism could be created."[13]

THE AVOWED AGRICULTURAL POLICY OF FASCISM

In 1919-20, when Mussolini's Blackshirts were still seeking a popular following, they joined with the left-wing parties in demanding division of the land among the peasants. Mussolini wrote in August 1919: "We demand expropriation of the land, the mines, and the transportation system. We support completely and absolutely the just demands of the peasants, miners, railroad workers, and sailors."[14] And the Fascist party program published in October 1920, called for confiscation of landed estates in the interests of the peasants.[15] In March 1921, the Duce could still promise (though with a significant qualification): "Within a few months all Italy will be in our power, and then we shall complete the agrarian revolution, which must give—in various ways suggested by the different regional conditions—the land to those that work on it."[16] By the end of 1921, however, insistence on outright division of the estates had quite given way to a modest proposal for "the diffusion of small holdings in all districts where agricultural and other conditions render them suitable and likely to be productive."[17] And after the "March on Rome" it was decided that if the number of proprietors were to be

[13] In a letter to Michele Bianchi, written August 27, 1921. See Mussolini, *Fascism: Doctrine and Institutions*, pp. 33-34.

[14] *Popolo d'Italia*, August 8, 1919. He expressed himself in favor of expropriation of the large estates again in the *Popolo d'Italia*, May 21, 1920.

[15] See Seldes, *Sawdust Caesar*, Appendix I, p. 387.

[16] Mussolini, *L'agricoltura e i rurali*, p. 18.

[17] From the Fascist party program of December 1921. See Por, *Fascism*, Appendix II, p. xxiii.

increased at all, it must be for the purpose of augmenting "the number of those interested in the defense of property."[18] The large landowners were discovered to have "not only the right but also the Fascist duty to remain in their superior positions as leaders."[19] Thus, as the alliance between Fascists, landowners, and industrialists was welded, the party's official language became increasingly guarded and finally revealed a profound respect for the institutions of private property.

Once in power, the Fascist leaders were not slow in recognizing their obligations to the landlords and rich farmers whose money and arms had helped them to victory over the left-wing movement in the countryside.

Within three months after the "March on Rome," the various decrees providing for cession of land to coöperatives were repealed, and steps were taken to oust the peasants from estates that they had occupied;[20] a proposed law for division of the *latifondi* was withdrawn,[21] and the measures limiting rises in land rents and eviction of tenants were revoked.[22] Arrigo Serpieri, the leading agricultural economist of Fascist Italy, explained these actions as follows:

The national government is firmly decided that out of the awkward super-structure and horrible deformations of State interven-

[18] See Gorgolini, *Il Fascismo nella vita italiana*, p. 62.

[19] Pesce, *Contadini d'Italia*, p. 87.

[20] A decree of January 11, 1923, annulled the Visocchi decree and its several amendments and made illegal the occupations already recognized by the provincial commissions. In consequence, the seized lands—in many cases considerably improved by several years of cultivation on the part of the peasants—were restored to their old proprietors.

[21] On August 10, 1922, the Chamber of Deputies passed a bill that would have provided for expropriation of poorly cultivated *latifondi*, subject to the payment of compensation to the owners, and for final transference to small peasant cultivators. Before the bill could receive the approval of the Senate, however, the Fascists "marched" on Rome. See Beals, "Absenteeism, Kissed and Crowned."

[22] Under the terms of a law of December 3, 1922, and of a decree of September 10, 1923.

tion the alert and lucid mechanism of private production must reappear. Free private enterprise, despite all the cries against its injustices, imperfections, and frictions, has been shown in the light of experience to be superior to State control, to "rational" regulation and "equitable" distribution imposed by public authority.[23]

But adherence to the principles of free enterprise was short-lived. It was not long before the Fascist government itself began to develop "State controls," to engage in "rational regulation" and "equitable distribution." However, the agricultural policy of Fascism, both in the first years when it reflected the spirit of *laissez-faire* and later when it required extensive government intervention, has continually been directed in the interests of landed property, commercialized agriculture, and finance capital.

This, of course, is not the admitted goal. On the contrary, Italian Fascism frequently masquerades in peasant dress. Thus, Mussolini tells the peasants:

I am proud to be your friend, your brother, your leader. . . . The Government looks on the peasants, in war and in peace, as the fundamental forces on which the country relies for its success. . . . As between the city and the village, I am for the village. . . . The time for a prevalently urban policy has passed. . . . The people who abandon the land are condemned to decadence. . . . I have willed that agriculture take first place in the Italian economy.[24]

Not only have the peasants been given a seat in the councils of the nation, but their interests are to be paramount. For Italy is to be "ruralized."[25]

[23] Serpieri, *La politica agraria in Italia*, p. 215.

[24] See Mussolini, *L'agricoltura e i rurali*, pp. 109-10; Serpieri and Mazzocchi-Alemanni, *Lo Stato fascista e i rurali, passim;* Longobardi, *Land Reclamation in Italy*, p. 176. Serpieri points out (in Mussolini, *op. cit.*, p. 11): "When the Duce speaks it is well for ordinary men to keep still."

[25] "To 'ruralize' means to hold the peasants to the soil, or, if they have

The Duce declares: "Italy must be ruralized, even if it costs billions and takes half a century."[26] A high degree of rurality means a rapidly growing population, healthy and strong, physically and morally. The rural life is the true, the good life, and develops the virtues of hard work and thrift. Moreover, it furnishes the nation's vital means of subsistence. It is dangerous for the nation, in the present period of history, to depend too much on the outside world for its prime necessities. Therefore, the casual wageworkers are to be given a stake in the land by being converted into share-croppers and tenants; the tenants and small proprietors are to be protected and increased in numbers. Agricultural production is to be vigorously encouraged, with special emphasis on intensive cultivation. Above all, the nation is to be made self-sufficient in its most essential foodstuff, wheat.

Furthermore, large areas of newly reclaimed land are to be made available to peasant colonists, thus providing room at home for the land-hungry masses and also enlarging the nation's productive capacity. The extensively cultivated estates must eventually, under pressure of competition from the favored intensive peasant farms, be split up voluntarily by their owners. However, all property rights—the fundamentals of social order—must be respected. Therefore, proposals for general expropriation of the large estates are rejected.[27] Only the failure of a proprietor to fulfill his "social duty" is just cause for his expropriation. Fascism seeks the goal of "class collaboration," in the country as well as in the towns. This is to be achieved by the subordination of indi-

left it, to bring them back to it." A. Marescalchi, a leading Fascist official, in *Sole,* March 23, 1930.

[26] Mussolini, *L'agricoltura e i rurali,* p. 87.

[27] "Also with regard to the *latifondisti,* Fascism respects private property rights." Serpieri and Mortara, "Politica agraria fascista," p. 246.

vidual interests to those of the nation, under the guidance of the Corporate State.[28]

Such, in general terms, are the pretensions of Fascist rural policy. But its reality can be discovered only in its practical application. The exposition of that reality is attempted in the following pages.

[28] "The Italian Nation is an organism endowed with a purpose, a life, and means of action transcending those of the individuals, or groups of individuals, composing it. . . . From the national standpoint, the whole body of production is a single unit; it has one single object—namely, the well being of the individuals and the development of national power." The Charter of Labor, paragraphs 1 and 2.

For detailed accounts of the avowed agricultural policy of Fascism, see Serpieri and Mazzocchi-Alemanni, *Lo Stato Fascista e i rurali;* Serpieri and Mortara, "Politica agraria fascista"; Mussolini, *L'agricoltura e i rurali;* Serpieri, *La politica agraria in Italia;* Serpieri, *Fra politica ed economia rurale;* Ministero dell'Economia Nazionale, *Il fascismo e l'agricoltura;* Ministero dell'Agricoltura e delle Foreste, *I progressi dell'agricoltura italiana in regime fascista.*

IV: The Battle for Bread

The rural policy of the Fascist government has enabled the Italian agricultural population to take a remarkable step forward.

—MUSSOLINI[1]

WHEAT is a commodity of fundamental importance in the Italian economy. It is the primary foodstuff of the people and is a staple crop throughout the country, in all regions and on every type of farm. Almost a fourth of the cultivated area is devoted to its production.[2]

Until near the end of the last century, Italy's output of wheat was sufficient to satisfy most of her needs. Industrialization, a rapidly growing population, and rising living standards, however, expanded wheat requirements. Domestic production did not keep pace, and increasing amounts had to be imported. The gap between needs and output broadened markedly during and immediately after the World War.

The population rose from 26,801,000 in 1871 to 34,814,000 in 1911, and to 36,836,000 in 1921 (within pre-War frontiers). During this period, domestic wheat production increased at about the same rate as the population. Average annual output was approximately 35,000,000 quintals in the

[1] Serpieri and Mazzocchi-Alemanni, *Lo Stato fascista e i rurali.*

[2] The annual per capita consumption of wheat flour and of alimentary pastes during 1926-34 was, respectively, 119.5 kilograms and 15.5 kilograms, among the highest in the world. Istituto Centrale di Statistica, *Annuario Statistico, 1936,* p. 139. The area under wheat is about 35 per cent of the total sown area of Italy (a greater proportion than in any other European country). The production of other cereals and potatoes is relatively unimportant. The dominating position of wheat culture is even more striking in view of the largely mountainous and hilly nature of the country.

decade 1872-81, 50,000,000 in 1905-14, and, after a contraction during the War, was again 50,000,000 in 1921-24. But per capita consumption rose so much (in consequence of the substitution of wheat bread and pastes for corn, chestnuts, and other foods) that, whereas a yearly average of only 3,000,000 quintals of foreign wheat was required in 1872-81, 13,000,000 were imported in 1905-14, and 26,000,000 in 1921-24.[3] By the beginning of the War, wheat had become the leading item among Italy's imports. In the immediate post-War period, imported wheat represented 15 to 20 per cent of the value of all imports.

Moreover, there was every prospect of continued rapid population growth, and Italy, already dependent on other countries for basic industrial raw materials, seemed likely to become also heavily dependent on foreign sources for its most essential food. To many people this situation caused concern. The rising wheat imports, occurring at a time of diminished emigrant remittances and tourist expenditures, added to the difficulties arising out of Italy's unfavorable foreign trade balance. Then too, the War had clearly revealed the seriousness of her dependence on overseas countries for coal, cotton, oil, and wheat. Any power or group of powers commanding the entrances to the Mediterranean could in such circumstances control the destiny of Italy. Thus, the conviction spread that every effort must be made to develop a greater degree of economic independence, in primary foodstuffs at any rate.[4]

[3] *Ibid.*, various years. It is to be noted, however, that the statistics of wheat production before 1910 are not reliable.

[4] The idea of a campaign for increased wheat production was not unknown before 1925. A nine-year series of competitions for improved wheat production in the Agro Romano began in 1914. In the crop year 1920-21 a national wheat propaganda campaign took place under government aus-

INITIATION OF THE "BATTLE OF WHEAT"

More immediate factors, however, lay behind the sudden decision of the Fascist government in the middle of 1925 to launch a vigorous program to raise the Italian wheat output.

The wheat harvest of 1923 was exceptionally good (many observers hastened to attribute this to the "social order" and "discipline" established by the new Fascist regime), but it was followed by a very poor crop in 1924. This led to heavy imports, high prices, and an unfavorable trade balance of record proportions.[5] The consequent threat to the Italian currency—already inflated—aroused grave concern in ruling circles. A reduction of the import excess would be necessary if the currency were to be stabilized. But wheat was the only major import commodity that could be produced in appreciably greater quantities at home. A high duty would stimulate increased domestic production, reduce consumption, and make possible a larger measure of independence of foreign supplies. A factor in the decision may also have been the benefits that the big landowners and chemical and machinery industrialists, who had been so important in helping the Fascists to power, would derive from a wheat tariff and from propaganda for increased use of fertilizer and agricultural machinery.

Considerations of a more purely political nature doubtless played a part as well. The Matteotti crisis in the second half of 1924 had severely shaken the prestige of the Fascist government. An aggressive and well-publicized wheat campaign,

---

pices. Proposals for compulsory wheat production on fallow or little-cultivated lands were also made in this period. Mussolini's newspaper, the *Popolo d'Italia*, in 1923 started a national wheat competition, which was continued for two years under private sponsorship.

[5] See Tables 1 and 2, below.

which would make a strong sentimental appeal to all patriotic Italians, might help to restore confidence in the regime and to direct public attention away from the issues raised by the murder of the Socialist deputy.

The manner in which the "Battle" was begun indicates that it was hastily decided upon, because of economic and political considerations of the moment. The hope prevailed that satisfactory results would be obtained in a short time—four or five years at most.[6] There is little evidence that the "Battle" was originally conceived as merely the first engagement in a farsighted campaign for the general intensification of agricultural production, a claim made by Fascist publicists in more recent years.

At any rate, the goal was clear from the beginning: to make Italy independent of foreign wheat in the shortest possible time, by means of a substantial rise in home production. This goal might be reached by increasing the area under wheat or by intensifying cultivation on the existing area. But the rational limit of wheat acreage had already been overstepped. Indeed, experts for years had been insisting that a drastic reduction of the grain areas would benefit Italian agriculture. Little in the way of a satisfactory rise in production, therefore, could be expected from acreage extension. Intensification was, however, another matter. Here the general conviction that much of Italy's farm land is irrationally cultivated, and that chemical fertilization, greater use of machinery, and seed selection can do much to raise its level of efficiency, gave rise to a definite hope. From the first, then, the official slogan was: "Intensified cultivation, but not increased acreage!"

[6] Mussolini, in his speech inaugurating the Permanent Wheat Committee, fixed its life at only three years.

METHODS

In the spring of 1925 the Duce sketched the main lines of the "Battle"; on June 20 he announced his purpose to the Chamber, and on July 4 the first meeting of the Permanent Wheat Committee took place. Thereafter a long series of measures were adopted by the government for the direction and prosecution of the campaign. In general terms, their aims were: (1) administration of the forces engaged in the "Battle," (2) direct stimulation of more intensive cultivation, and (3) support of domestic wheat prices.[7]

The Permanent Wheat Committee was the central administrative organ in the campaign. Its function was to supervise the progress of the "Battle," to study means whereby wheat production might be increased, and to make recommendations to the government.[8] Local official and semiofficial agencies, including provincial wheat commissions, agricultural-workers' and employers' syndicates, coöperatives, and educational bodies, were entrusted with the task of administering the program in the provinces and communes.

Directly to encourage more intensive cultivation a variety of subsidy devices were developed. Most important among these were reduction of the price of gasoline used in farm

[7] For a detailed account and general critique of the campaign, see Müller-Einhart, *Mussolinis Getreideschlacht*. Other analyses: Vöchting, "Die italienische Getreideschlacht"; Salvemini, "Mussolini's Battle of Wheat"; Ucker, *Die italienische Agrarpolitik seit 1925*. Most Italian accounts are too uncritical, too bent on slavishly praising the Fascist regime, to be of value.

[8] The composition of the Committee has been changed several times. At present, it consists of the Duce as chairman; representatives of the Fascist Party, the ministries of agriculture, corporations and finance, the cereals corporation, the confederations of agricultural workers and employers, the syndicate of agricultural technicians; and a number of experts. In all, it has twenty-four members.

machines and of railroad freight rates for chemical fertilizers; money to encourage the development of farm machinery suitable to Italian conditions; aid in the distribution of selected seeds, the construction of silos, and the adoption of seed-sorting machines, motor-ploughs, and other machines; subsidization of reclamation projects, building of roads, stalls, troughs, and the like, on land adaptable to wheat. Technical education and research were also encouraged: added financial help was given to experimental institutes, agricultural schools, and to the system of agricultural advisers;[9] local committees were established for the operation of demonstration fields.

At the same time, propaganda weapons, wielded by newspapers, schools, churches, radios, motor caravans, were employed to foster "wheat consciousness" in the nation. Intensive efforts were made to instill in the peasants and farmers an eagerness for victory in the "Battle." Yearly wheat-growing competitions—both national and local—were sponsored, and astonishingly high yields were obtained by the winners. In 1932 a record yield of 73 quintals per hectare was obtained on a 20-hectare field; the maximum in 1933 was 88.3 quintals per hectare on two hectares. The government thus was able to arouse widespread interest in the progress of the "Battle" in the cities as well as in the countryside.[10]

Quite the most important tactic in the campaign, however, was the maintenance of Italian wheat prices above world-market levels, with the effect of at once stimulating production and checking consumption. The government continually worked to this end, chiefly by means of a high duty on imports.

[9] The *Cattedre Ambulenti di Agricoltura.*

[10] See Müller-Einhart, *Mussolinis Getreideschlacht*, pp. 20-53. But these efforts to arouse enthusiasm were less effective in the traditionally backward South than in the North.

In effect, the "Battle" was opened with the reintroduction on July 24, 1925 of a tariff of 7.50 gold lire per quintal of wheat.[11] Thereafter, the tariff was raised as follows: on September 12, 1928, to 11 gold lire; on May 23, 1929, to 14 gold lire; on June 4, 1930, to 16 gold lire, and finally on August 16, 1931, to 75 paper lire (roughly equivalent to 19 gold lire). Since the beginning of 1935, wheat imports have been under strict quota control. Heavy duties on wheat flour, corn, and other competitive cereals and cereal products also were imposed. The poor crop of 1936, and the consequent necessity of importing substantial quantities of wheat at rising world prices, required tariff reductions in order to avoid marked advances in bread prices. The duty was lowered to 47 lire on October 6, 1936, to 32 lire on October 30, and to 18 lire on January 30, 1937.

But the weakness of wheat prices after 1928-29 necessitated recourse to additional price-supporting devices.[12]

In order to prevent the accumulation by millers of large stores of foreign wheat, which might make possible downward pressure on domestic prices, compulsory mixing regulations were introduced in 1931. These require that in the milling of flour a minimum percentage of domestic wheat be mixed with the foreign products.[13] Also, specifications for bread and other wheat products were defined for the purpose of discouraging consumption of fine flours (largely of foreign origin).

Characteristic of the Italian wheat market in the past was

[11] The unpopular pre-War duty of 7.50 lire per quintal had been suspended early in 1915.

[12] The government has also undertaken to reduce costs of production, especially by cutting wages of agricultural labor.

[13] The milling regulations have been changed from time to time. The required percentage of home-grown wheat has risen as high as 99.

a decided seasonal price decline directly after the harvest, a consequence of immediate sale of a large proportion of the crop by producers in need of money or lacking storage facilities. To prevent these gluts and to enable the farmers to obtain a larger share of the final wheat price, adequate storage and credit facilities were necessary. This need has been met, in large measure, by the development under government auspices of a system of wheat pools, credit advances, and collective sales. For this purpose the construction of warehouses and silos were subsidized. Beginning in 1936 the pooling for collective sale of all market wheat was made obligatory.[14]

These measures, together with the controls over enterprise exerted under the corporative system, have enabled the government in recent years practically to fix wheat prices. Indeed, the entire domestic cereals market is now dominated by the corporative organs of the government. Various agencies determine the necessary imports of each kind and quality of cereals, assign the import quotas to a single organization (the Federation of Agricultural Marketing Coöperatives), and control prices and internal distribution. Prices, not only of cereals and cereal products, but also of other commodities, have been under the continual surveillance of a special Fascist party committee, and, more recently, of the Central Corporative Committee.[15]

While it has not been possible to prevent a nominal price

[14] The amount of wheat pooled and sold collectively rose from 215,000 quintals in 1930 to about 8,000,000 in 1935. (The pools are much more important in the North than in the South.) In consequence, the seasonal price fluctuations were reduced. See Pareschi, "Gli ammassi collettivi di grano e la loro organizzazione," pp. 5-7; Mortara, *Prospettive Economiche, 1935*.

[15] See *La Tribuna* (Rome), June 16, 1936; Fascist Confederation of Industrialists, *Business and Financial Report*, May 1937.

TABLE 1

PRICES OF WHEAT ON THE ITALIAN MARKETS[16]

1923-35

Annual unweighted averages; current lire per quintal

CROP YEARS	FOREIGN WHEAT (IMPORT PRICE LESS DUTY)	DOMESTIC WHEAT	PURCHASING POWER OF DOMESTIC WHEAT
1923–24	102	100	100
1924–25	156	163	85
1925–26	163	195	126
1926–27	156	172	137
1927–28	110	132	137
1928–29	100	131	126
1929–30	93	131	136
1930–31	64	111	131
1931–32	49	107	140
1932–33	46	103	146
1933–34	41	85	129
1934–35	37	94	137

decline since 1925-26, the gap between domestic and foreign prices has continually broadened and the purchasing power of wheat in the home market has actually risen.

RESULTS IN TERMS OF WHEAT PRODUCTION

The immediate goal of the "Battle"—virtual self-sufficiency in wheat—has been closely approached.

Throughout the period of the campaign the total *area* under wheat tended to rise.[17] During the five years 1931-35 it averaged about 5,000,000 hectares, roughly 300,000 hectares above

[16] Prices of foreign and domestic wheat from Mortara, *Prospettive Economiche*, *1932*, p. 58; *1935*, p. 415. Purchasing power index based on all-commodity wholesale price index and prices of domestic non-durum wheat.

[17] The year-to-year fluctuations in area followed closely the changes in purchasing power.

Table 2

ACREAGE, YIELD, PRODUCTION, AND NET IMPORTS OF WHEAT[18]

1909-14—1921-36

YEAR	AREA (MILLIONS OF HECTARES)	YIELD (QUINTALS PER HECTARE)	PRODUCTION (MILLIONS OF QUINTALS)	NET IMPORTS[a] (MILLIONS OF QUINTALS)
1909-14 (Annual average)	4.76	10.35	49.3	14.5
1921	4.8	11.0	52.5	26.3
1922	4.7	9.5	44.0	31.4
1923	4.7	13.1	61.2	20.9
1924	4.6	10.1	46.3	25.7
1925	4.7	13.9	65.5	16.3
1926	4.92	12.2	60.1	20.9
1927	4.98	10.8	53.3	23.7
1928	4.96	12.5	62.2	23.6
1929	4.77	14.8	70.8	11.2
1930	4.82	11.9	57.2	21.9
1931	4.81	13.8	66.5	8.7
1932	4.93	15.3	75.4	3.4
1933	5.09	16.0	81.3	3.1
1934	4.97	12.8	63.4	2.8
1935	5.03	15.4	77.1	1.2
1936	5.13	11.8	61.0	8.4[b]

[a] From August 1 of the year indicated to July 31 of the next year. Net imports of wheat flour, semolina, and wheat paste are included; coefficients of conversion into wheat equivalents are, respectively, .73, .65, .72.

[b] To April 30, 1937. Preliminary estimates point to total net imports of 14,000,000 quintals in the crop year 1936-37. But the 1937 harvest is expected to exceed 80,000,000 quintals. New York *Times*, July 19, 1937.

---

[18] Istituto Centrale di Statistica, *Annuario Statistico*, various issues, and *Bollettino Mensile di Statistica Agraria*, October 1925, p. 916. These production data are not wholly reliable. Changes in methods of threshing and estimating crops seem to have made for "statistical" increases after 1925. In discussing the system of compulsory wheat pools, the National Confederation of Industrialists, *Business and Financial Report* (February 1937) notes that "the new system will allow of collection for the first time

that in 1921-25.[19] Most of this increase occurred at the expense of hillside pasture in the peninsular South, Sicily, and Sardinia, regions in which the wheat area has always been extensive. In those regions, the average wheat area in 1931-35 was 13 per

TABLE 3

ANNUAL AVERAGE WHEAT YIELDS[20]

1909-14, 1921-35

Quintals per hectare

PERIODS	NORTH ITALY	CENTRAL ITALY	SOUTH ITALY AND ISLANDS
1909–14	14.5	9.1	8.1
1921–25	16.5	9.9	8.9
1926–30	17.2	11.1	10.1
1931–35	21.8	13.7	10.7

cent higher than in 1921-25. In North and Central Italy the new acreage was insignificant.[21]

National average *yields*, rising already before the initiation

---

of really reliable statistics on production, stocks and consumption of [wheat]."

[19] This rise, even though relatively slight, took place against the express wishes of the government. Skeptical observers are inclined to believe that local officials, desiring to respect the government's wishes, frequently underestimated the acreage.

[20] See W. Busse, "Getreidefeldzug und Weizenerzeugung in Italien," p. 29; Istituto Centrale di Statistica, *Bollettino Mensile di Statistica*, *Bollettino Mensile di Statistica Agraria*, various numbers, 1926-35.

[21] Wheat areas (annual averages in 1,000 hectares, exclusive of territories acquired since the World War):

	North Italy	*Central Italy*	*South Italy and Islands*
1909–14	1,436	1,019	2,305
1921–25	1,407	1,046	2,191
1926–30	1,412	1,040	2,401
1931–35	1,478	1,041	2,465

Same sources as in footnote 20, this chapter.

of the "Battle," advanced unsteadily but appreciably after 1925. The average in 1931-35 was 14.6 quintals per hectare, as compared with 12.4 in 1926-30, 11.5 in 1921-25, and 10.4 in 1909-14.[22] Here again, there are notable differences between the various regions. (See Table 3.)

Thus, yields in North and Central Italy rose about 50 per cent between 1909-14 and 1931-35, but only 32 per cent in the South.

Production in the first phase of the campaign was disappointingly low from the official point of view, averaging only 60,700,000 quintals per year in 1926-30 as against 53,900,000 in 1921-25. Such increase as occurred then was probably more the result of favorable weather and of acreage extension than anything else.[23] Significant results could never have been reasonably expected in these first years; some time was necessary before the capital, technique, and labor invested during the campaign could bear fruit.

The government was, however, unwilling to admit this. It celebrated the good crops as the result of its policies, and blamed bad weather for the poor crops. Appeal was frequently made to the so-called "dynamic law of wheat production," according to which a good crop year is generally followed by a

[22] Yields had been rising for at least 40 years before the War. They averaged only 8.4 quintals per hectare in 1871-75—25 per cent below those of 1909-14.

[23] The influence of the weather is suggested by comparison with wheat yields (quintals per hectare) in neighboring countries:

	1925	*1926*	*1927*	*1928*	*1929*	*1930*	*1931*
Italy	13.9	12.2	10.8	12.5	14.8	11.9	13.8
France	16.0	12.0	14.2	14.6	17.0	11.6	13.8
Spain	10.2	9.1	9.0	7.8	9.8	8.9	9.0

(Data taken from International Institute of Agriculture, *International Yearbook of Agricultural Statistics*, various years.)

bad one. Nevertheless, official statisticians were for some years embarrassed by the large crops of 1923 and 1925. The 1923 crop (coming in the first year of the Fascist "era") was originally hailed as almost a divine judgment in favor of the new regime. Likewise, the harvest of 1925, occurring just after the initiation of the "Battle," was considered the first triumph of the campaign. But the next three seasons were poor, and hardly convincing evidence of the promised early "wheat victory." Thereupon official sources admitted that the crop of 1925 had been overestimated in the first flush of the "Battle." Also, it was decided that the estimate for 1926 had been too large.[24]

After 1930 more satisfactory results were obtained. Output in the period 1931-35 averaged 72,700,000 quintals, markedly higher than ever obtained before, even in the best crop years. Average production in the five *best* years before the beginning of the "Battle" (1911, 1913, 1921, 1923, 1925) was 58,000,000 quintals—that is, 20 per cent less than the average of 1931-35. Wheat crops in recent years have been fully 40 per cent larger than before the War, whereas acreage has increased only about 4 per cent. Roughly nine-tenths of the increased production is attributable to the higher yields. Comparison with other countries also gives some indication of the Italian progress. As against average yields in 1909-13, the average in 1930-34 was 32 per cent higher in Italy, 27 per cent higher in France, 2 per cent higher in Spain, 5 per cent higher in Great Britain and Northern Ireland, and about 0.5 per cent higher in Germany. But Italian yields are still below those of France, and far below those of England and Ger-

[24] Mortara (*Prospettive economiche, 1929,* p. 32) reduces the harvest of 1925 from 65,500,000 quintals to 63,000,000, and that of 1926 from 60,100,000 to 55,000,000. This, of course, makes the 1927 harvest seem less unfavorable. Official publications, however, still give the original figures.

many.[25] However, the hilly character of much of Italy's wheat land and the fact that much wheat is cultivated together with vines and trees must be kept in mind in making such comparisons.

This increase was partly responsible for a drastic reduction of imports, at least during 1931-35, and a marked approach toward self-sufficiency. But, as will be shown below, a substantial decline in the consumption of wheat products was also a factor in this attainment.

Thus, in terms of its immediate objectives the "Battle of Wheat" has been substantially victorious. Indeed, it is difficult to understand how, in view of the extraordinary means adopted, such an ultimate victory could ever have been in doubt. But it has been purchased at the cost of seriously unbalancing Italian agriculture and of imposing a heavy burden on workers and consumers.

RATIONALIZATION OF AGRICULTURE AND THE PROBLEM OF THE SOUTH

Fascist commentators frequently present the "Wheat Battle" as symbolic of a program for the intensification of agricultural production in general. Closer examination of recent developments in Italian agriculture shows that this claim has little foundation. During the first five or six years of the campaign, at least, commodities other than wheat were relatively neglected.

Of course, the official pressure for the adoption of more rational methods of cultivation—deep ploughing, seed selection, sowing in rows, use of chemical fertilizers—has raised the technical level of wheat production. It has also had indirect

[25] Based on data in the International Institute of Agriculture, *International Yearbook of Agricultural Statistics*, various years.

effect on agricultural methods in general, at least on the Northern commercialized farms. Per hectare yields of other grains and of potatoes have risen, especially in the North.[26] Some of these gains are attributable to the increased use of fertilizers and machinery. The approximate annual average consumption of all chemical fertilizers was 12,000,000 quintals in 1910-14, 11,000,000 in 1919-25, and 17,000,000 in 1926-31; it has decreased slightly since 1931. In 1924, 5,840 farm tractors were in use; this number rose to 23,662 in 1931.[27] Much attention has also been paid to the development of select strains of wheat, particularly to early-ripening varieties suitable to the South. The use of select seeds has been increasing steadily; it is claimed that the area sown to such seed rose from about 15 per cent of the total wheat area in 1924-25 to 63 per cent in 1934. But all these gains have been much less pronounced in the southern provinces than in the northern. The land-tenure system and the poverty of the South have not admitted noteworthy technical advances. Furthermore, the peculiarities of southern soil and climate operate against effective application of chemical fertilizers, deep ploughing, and machinery.[28]

[26] Average annual yields (quintals per hectare) in the four periods 1909-13, 1921-25, 1926-30, 1931-35, were, respectively: corn, 15.8, 15.7, 16.0, 20.2; rye, 11.8, 12.4, 13.2, 13.9; barley, 8.9, 9.6, 10.2, 10.9; oats, 10.6, 11.4, 11.7, 12.5; rice, 32.8, 42.0, 47.1, 48.5; potatoes, 57.6, 52.9, 55.9, 59.3. Istituto Centrale di Statistica, *Annuario Statistico*, various years.

[27] G. Raineri, "Fertilizzanti e Macchine," in Federzoni, *I problemi attuali dell'agricoltura italiana*, pp. 319 ff.

[28] In 1932, 135.4 kilograms of phosphatic fertilizers and 75.7 kilograms of nitrates were applied to each hectare under wheat in North Italy; the respective amounts for Central Italy are 108.9 and 37.3; for the South, 26.1 and 11.9. Serpieri and Mazzocchi-Alemanni, *Lo Stato fascista e i rurali*, p. 144. For doubts in respect to the techniques promoted under the wheat campaign, see Müller-Einhart, *Mussolinis Getreideschlacht*, pp. 164 ff.; Vöchting, "Die italienische Getreideschlacht," pp. 34 ff.

But continual emphasis on more and yet more wheat production; the slight attention given by the technical advisers to rotation, animal husbandry, and general farm management; the greater purchasing power of wheat in consequence of tariff protection—all tended to draw attention away from other important branches of agriculture. Tree crops and live stock probably have suffered most from the one-sidedness of the wheat policy.

Italy is by nature excellently adapted to the production of fruits, vegetables, nuts, and vines. The mild Mediterranean climate and the soil permit the growing not only of most temperate fruits and vegetables, but also of many subtropical plants. Because of the great extension of the country from north to south, it is possible to distribute vegetable harvests over most of the year.

Thus, Italy has peculiar advantages as a supplier of southern fruits, wines, and early vegetables to European markets. Certainly the export of these commodities is important. But Italy did not share in the increased world trade of predepression years as did other countries, including its closest competitor, Spain. Annual average exports of citrus fruits, olive oil, and wine from Italy and Spain were:[29]

		1909–13	*1925–29*	*1930–34*
Oranges and mandarins	Italy	1199.6	1215.1	1095.4
	Spain	5078.6	7406.7	9366.2
Lemons	Italy	2669.0	2339.7	2593.2
	Spain	33.1	159.0	227.4
Olive oil	Italy	306.2	293.8	22.0[a]
	Spain	392.0	748.3	718.5
Wine	Italy	1525.8	1059.4	1084.9
	Spain	3103.3	4138.4	2575.3

[a] Net import.

[29] Based on data in International Institute of Agriculture, *International Yearbook of Agricultural Statistics*, various years.

Spain's share of world citrus exports amounted to 47 per cent in 1909-13, 47 per cent in 1925-29, 52 per cent in 1930-33. Italy's share in these three periods was, respectively, 36 per cent, 22 per cent, and 21 per cent.

Methods of cultivation, harvesting, packing, and transport have lagged behind, and costs of production have remained high. If anything like the attention paid to wheat had been given to these crops, no doubt substantial progress could have been made. In more recent years some efforts have been made to improve the marketing of fruits, vegetables, and wines. Yet the situation of the fruit industry continues to be critical. Cultivation, particularly of citrus fruits, has deteriorated, for growers cannot afford to maintain orchards. Cultivation of grapes has also fallen.

More serious has been the decline of the live-stock industry, which has long been backward both in extent and methods.[30] Experts have repeatedly advocated support of this industry as a policy well calculated to strengthen the country's agriculture. But since the beginning of the wheat campaign there has been a general reduction of the farm-animal population—astonishingly severe in some regions. The following table presents a vivid picture of that reduction. It gives the numbers of animals in 1918, 1926, 1930, and 1936 as percentages of those in 1908.[31]

[30] The average number of cattle throughout the country is only 21.8 per square kilometer, and falls to 7.9 in the South and Islands.

[31] Animals with the army, in the royal stables, on railways, and in the former Austrian territories are not included. Sources: Ministero di Agricoltura, Industria e Commercio, *Censimento generale del bestiame del 19 marzo 1908*; Ministero per l'Agricoltura, *Censimento generale del bestiame nel 1918*; N. Fottichia, "L'industria zootecnica," in Federzoni, *I problemi attuali dell'agricoltura italiana*, p. 273; Istituto Centrale di Statistica, *Censimento generale del bestiame al 19 marzo 1930*; Istituto Centrale di Statistica, *Annuario Statistico, 1937*, p. 56.

	Horses, Asses and Mules	Cattle	Hogs	Sheep	Goats
Census of 1908	100	100	100	100	100
Census of 1918	96	100	92	105	114
Official estimate of 1926	120	120	114	111	115
Census of 1930	105	106	126	90	67
Official estimate of 1936	95	117	126	79	66

In absolute figures, the animal population in 1936 was (in thousands): horses, asses, and mules, 2,043; cattle (including buffaloes), 7,235; hogs, 3,206; sheep, 8,862; goats, 1,795.

The live-stock reduction has not been uniform in all parts of the country. In the northern and central *compartimenti,* the number of horses, asses, mules, cattle, and hogs rose between 1918 and 1930, while that of goats and sheep fell. In the *Mezzogiorno,* however, the reduction in all groups except horses, asses, and mules has been drastic. Between 1918 and 1930 the declines were: cattle, 20 per cent; hogs, 10 per cent; sheep, 18 per cent; goats, 38 per cent. The number of horses, asses, and mules rose about 7 per cent. The 1930 census revealed such startling losses that re-counts were made in certain provinces. By 1936 the South had suffered a further loss of 11 per cent of its animal population, while the reduction in North and Central Italy was only 2 per cent.

Major responsibility for these unfavorable developments must be assigned to the government's wheat policy. The heavy duties on wheat and competing grains upset the balance between the various branches of agricultural production. Italian livestock producers, laboring under high costs of grain and fodders (much higher than in the Danubian countries, from which come most of the animals imported into Italy), could not withstand the increased competition of cheaply produced foreign meats. Moreover, the wheat program made it profitable to convert natural pasture into wheat fields. (As noted above, most of the recent increases in wheat area took place at the expense of pasture areas in the South.) The higher rents of pasture land particularly damaged the sheep industry. Heavy taxes on goats (the "cows of the poor") and on meat consumption have also been a depressing factor.

Imports of live animals, butter, and wool rose markedly after 1925. Eggs, once a significant export, are now imported. Italy's dependence on foreign sources of animal products has thus increased.

ITALY'S FOREIGN TRADE IN LIVE STOCK, ANIMAL PRODUCTS, AND COTTON[32]

Annual averages; import surplus indicated as +; export surplus as —

	1909–13	1925–29	1930–34
Large cattle (1,000 head)	+ 32.3	+ 71.4	+ 102.8
Calves (1,000 head)	+ 47.8	+ 55.8	+ 36.0
Hogs (1,000 head)	— 8.7	— 11.8	— 264.0[a]
Fresh, chilled and frozen meats (1,000 quintals)	+ 57.2	+ 673.3	+ 480.1
Butter (1,000 quintals)	— 31.3	+ 6.9[b]	+ 12.5
Cheese (1,000 quintals)	— 214.3	— 301.0	— 265.6
Eggs (1,000 quintals)	— 199.9	— 53.6	+ 151.3
Wool (1,000 quintals)	+ 118.9	+ 417.0	+ 630.7
Cotton (1,000 quintals)	+1941.7	+2321.9	+1943.5[c]

[a] Probably includes a large number of foreign hogs in transit through Italy.

[b] Average of 1927-29.

[c] Note that cotton imports were declining at the same time as wool imports were rising.

It is South Italy, above all, that has borne the burden of overemphasis on wheat cultivation and neglect of other industries.

[32] Data from International Institute of Agriculture, *International Yearbook of Agricultural Statistics*, various years.

As noted above, the increase in wheat output during the course of the "Battle" was much less marked in the South than in the North. Not only did the Southern regions remain behind in production techniques, but wide fluctuations in output from year to year also continued.[33]

Low yields and close dependence on weather fluctuations, characteristic of wheat production in South Italy, are basically a function of natural conditions. The North, with its combination of ample rainfall and warmth during the spring and summer—that is, during the period of flowering and grain formation—is well adapted to the cultivation of wheat. On the other hand, the South has rainfall during the winter and long, hot, and dry summers, a soil poor in organic substance, and much hilly and mountainous land. That is, the physical conditions are hostile to efficient grain production.[34] The wheat monoculture practiced in much of the South is, in turn, hostile to the soil, tending to reduce its productivity. It has been well said of these regions that "the wheat of today eliminates the wheat of tomorrow." Nevertheless, nearly one-half of the total wheat area of Italy is in the South. This wide cultivation is explained to large extent by the desire of the many small peasant farmers to produce enough wheat for their own needs, regardless of peculiarities of soil, climate, or land elevation.

[33] For example, yields (in quintals per hectare) fluctuated in Apulia as follows: *1926*, 13.3; *1927*, 7.4; *1928*, 11.4; *1929*, 14.7; *1930*, 9.8. Throughout South Italy the relation between the amount of rain during the earing period and the size of the crop is close.

[34] Scarcity of moisture during the critical period of wheat development, high temperatures, and intense light are natural barriers to high wheat yields. The size of wheat crops therefore depends primarily on the course of the weather, and only secondarily on methods of cultivation. However, the practical development of early-ripening wheats may overcome some of these difficulties. Varieties have been produced which ripen two to three weeks before ordinary types and so can more often escape the damage caused by hot, dry winds in the period of grain formation.

But the southern climate is favorable to certain types of production, such as citrus fruits, vines, figs, olives, almonds, grasses, and forage plants. Furthermore, the manure of pasture animals and the soil-building clovers and beans would enrich the soil and make it ultimately more productive even in cereals. The old problem of backward techniques and low production in the *Mezzogiorno* would find a partial solution in the encouragement of fruit, vegetable, and nut cultivation and of animal husbandry, which are specifically suited to the natural character of the country. This would call for less, not more, wheat—not an intensification of grain cultivation, but rather a reorientation of the entire southern agricultural system. The "Battle of Wheat," then, by not only maintaining but also leading to an increase of wheat acreage and a decline of live stock has made even more pronounced the one-sidedness so often deplored by students of the problem of the South.

In more recent times, these errors of the wheat program have been tacitly admitted in official quarters. The government has shown increasing concern for the live-stock industry. High tariff duties on imports of animals and animal products were introduced in 1932. A national animal-husbandry competition was begun in 1930 and in 1934 the annual wheat contest was transformed into a "National Wheat and Farm Competition," which is intended to encourage not only higher wheat yields, but also more rational rotation and improvements in forage crops and live-stock breeding. In 1936, despite the poor wheat crop, there was relatively little official insistence on the need for greater production.

TARIFFS, WHEAT PRICES, AND CONSUMPTION

The fundamental measure in the campaign for increased wheat production was the adoption of heavy (and, during

1931-36, almost prohibitive) restrictions on wheat imports. Tariff protection for wheat has been described by Fascists as a compensation to the agricultural population for the burden of industrial protection. It is necessary to examine the relationships between landownership, wheat production, and marketing in order to determine the merits of this claim.

The extraordinarily large number of share-tenants and small peasant proprietors means that insofar as a wheat tariff is of help to agriculture, such help goes predominantly to the landowning class. It is only the proprietors of medium-sized farms and the large landowners, after all, who have substantial supplies of wheat available for market and who can thus profit from the price-supporting measures.[35] Share-tenants and smallholders themselves consume the bulk of their production and sometimes must even purchase wheat products to satisfy all their needs. It has been estimated that two-fifths of the Italian cereal production is directly consumed by the peasants. This means, too, that the development of collective pools has been of aid primarily to the larger wheat producers.[36] Indeed, the increasing organization of wheat marketing has narrowed the outlets for such small amounts of wheat as peasants may have for sale. Formerly, they were able to sell in village and town markets at going prices; now such markets have been greatly

[35] Whether deliberately or not, several of the rises in the duty helped large wheat producers, dealers, millers, and bakers considerably more than the small producers. The tariff increases of July 1925, September 1928, and August 1931 took place at a time when the greater part of the marketable production from small and medium-sized farms had already passed out of the hands of the farmers. The higher prices resulting from the new duties therefore were of advantage largely to the farmers able to finance the storage of their wheat (that is, the bigger landowners) and the middlemen.

[36] For instance, the 4,407,000 quintals of pooled wheat in 1934 were the property of only 60,848 producers—an average of about 72 quintals per person—predominantly of North Italy. Pareschi, "Gli ammassi collettivi."

reduced and they must dispose of their wheat to relatively few dealers and to large farmers at less favorable prices. The heavily indebted peasants frequently sell their disposable unharvested wheat at very low prices to their creditors. Furthermore, although the share-tenants generally have only small marketable quantities, they must divide the increased expenses of wheat cultivation equally with their landlords. That is, the higher costs burden them more heavily.

Thus the maldistribution of agricultural income is intensified. The capital so much needed by the poorer enterprises remains in the hands of non-operating, absentee owners.

Finally, the mass of agricultural wageworkers are interested in wheat essentially as consumers. For them, the tariff is only a factor in higher living costs—all the more burdensome because of the great importance of bread in their diet.[37]

The Fascist defense of the wheat tariff as a premium distributed among the rural masses must, then, be rejected. The majority of the agricultural population actually has been penalized by the wheat tariff as well as by industrial tariffs. The great army of industrial and agricultural wage earners, in whose food budgets bread and pastes play a major role, have been the cannon fodder of the "Wheat Battle." Their contribution has been in unnecessarily higher living costs and in reduced consumption.

In the years 1925-35 Italian consumers paid a premium on their wheat of roughly 32,000,000,000 lire—a premium that

[37] Because of widespread unemployment and the bargaining weaknesses of the Fascist labor organization, not only have the workers been unable to obtain a share of the tariff advantages through higher wages, but their incomes have also declined drastically during the period of the "Battle." It should be noted that increased wheat cultivation tends to raise unemployment, inasmuch as it often takes the place of crops that require considerably more labor.

benefited chiefly the large and medium-sized landowners.[38] That is, all the wheat available to consumers during this period could, in the absence of a tariff, have been bought for 69,180,000,000 lire; actually it cost 101,540,000,000 lire, almost 50 per cent more. According to Salvemini,[39] a family of workers consisting of man and wife and three children under 12 years consumes slightly less than 10 quintals (about 2,000 pounds) of wheat per year. The average annual excess cost on this amount has been about 400 lire, that is, 5 to 10 per cent of the total yearly earnings of many workers.

Also, no small part of the public funds has been spent on the campaign. Official sources admit that during the four financial years 1925-26 to 1928-29, 225,570,000 lire were provided for this purpose. By the end of 1936 the total cost may easily have been as much as 300,000,000 lire.[40]

Furthermore, consumption of wheat declined during the years of the campaign. The average quantity annually available per capita during the crop years *1909-13* was 166.1 kilograms; *1921-25*, 187 kilograms; *1926-30*, 182.8 kilograms; *1931-35*, 159.9 kilograms.[41] That is, the increase in domestic

[38] This is calculated by subtracting the total hypothetical cost (at import prices less duty) of the domestic wheat production and of net imports during this period from the actual cost. The annual excess cost has been, in billions of lire, in each crop season: *1925-26*, 2.7; *1926-27*, 1.71; *1927-28*, 1.84; *1928-29*, 2.90; *1929-30*, 3.27; *1930-31*, 4.03; *1931-32*, 4.40; *1932-33*, 4.34; *1933-34*, 3.62; *1934-35*, 3.55. The total of 32,360,000,000 lire is comprised of 6,130,000,000 in tariff charges and 26,230,000,000 of excess payments to domestic sellers. Based on data in Mortara, *Prospettive Economiche*, *1932*, *1935*.

[39] Salvemini, "Mussolini's Battle of Wheat."

[40] Ministry of Agriculture and Forests, *The Wheat Campaign in Italy*, Appendix A.

[41] This is estimated by adding net imports of wheat and wheat products to the total domestic production less seed, and dividing this sum by the current population figure (some 6,000,000 to 7,500,000 quintals are required yearly for seed). Inasmuch as there are no carryover data, it is impos-

production has not been sufficient to compensate for the reduced imports. Consequently consumption has fallen to levels lower than those known immediately before the World War. Thus, the price-supporting measures of the campaign have made for "self-sufficiency" both by raising production and by diminishing consumption. Consumers have suffered, indirectly, too, by reason of the relative neglect of other agricultural commodities.

THE UPSHOT

Shortly before the World War, Ghino Valenti (then the leading agricultural economist in Italy) wrote:

> The day when we limit ourselves to a cultivation of not more than three and a half million hectares of wheat, harvesting normally 70 million quintals, and at the same time raise a third more animals than now—on that day the equilibrium [of Italian agriculture] will be reestablished, and rural Italy will serve the needs of the nation by supplying it with the most essential foodstuffs and by enriching it with the exportation of those agricultural commodities that are a special prerogative of our soil and climate.[42]

The policy of the Fascist regime, running directly counter to this sound advice, has been irrational in terms of the best interests of Italian agriculture. The evils of wheat monoculture in the South have been perpetuated, little account has been

---

sible to estimate the apparent disappearance. Various signs, including preparations for the Abyssinian campaign, point to greatly increased stocks in recent years. If this is true, consumption was reduced even more than indicated above. Apparently consumption of *polenta* (corn meal mush) is on the increase, especially in the country districts. See also Table 8, p. 162.

[42] Quoted by Lenti, in "L'industria zootecnica italiana: Prospettive d'incremento e di miglioramento," p. 201. This is essentially the recommendation made by Italian agricultural economists since the days of Stefano Jacini. Another economist has declared: "I do not deny the possibility of our producing all the wheat we need, but I deny the desirability of our doing so, for in Italy too much badly adapted land is dedicated to wheat." Rivera, *Battaglie per il grano*, p. 112.

taken of the natural limitations and advantages of the country, and future productivity has been menaced. In consequence, important branches of agriculture have retrogressed. All of this outweighs the advances in agricultural techniques to which the "Wheat Battle" has contributed. Obviously the real basis of the campaign has been something other than a genuine desire to rationalize Italian agriculture.

With respect to the international trade balance, it is not enough to point only to the reduction in wheat imports. Account must also be taken of the greater imports of meats and wool and the reduced exports of fruits, oil, wines, eggs, and other products for which the wheat policy has been in part responsible. Moreover, the "Battle" took place at a time when world wheat prices were falling drastically. This decline, and the increased purchasing power of the lira on world markets, would have enabled Italy to import wheat very cheaply. The campaign, instead, raised costs of food and reduced export possibilities.

It may be argued that "Great Power" politics demand the development of self-sufficiency, even at the expense of immediately greater mass poverty and possible loss of foreign markets for Italian products (markets that are capricious in any case, in the present state of international relations). But even in terms of military necessity the "Battle" can have no more than limited effectiveness. A really determined blockade of the Mediterranean still could quickly and seriously embarrass the Italian economy, dependent as it is on foreign edible fats, petroleum, coal, iron, cotton, wool, and other materials. Some Italian economists have held, in fact, that a "battle *against* wheat" would be much more helpful in raising Italy's self-sufficiency in a period of emergency. If forage crops were substituted for wheat, then it would be possible to build up a reserve of meat animals and of enriched land capable of quick conversion into high-yielding grain fields.[43]

In broad terms, the "Battle of Wheat" has solely served the material welfare of the industrialist and landowning class.

The division of interests among the Italian people in respect of tariff policy—in fact, of economic policy in general—is clear-cut. The large and medium-sized landowners fear foreign competition in the wheat market, and have a definite interest in the erection of a protective tariff wall for wheat. Here they stand on common ground with the protectionist group of big machinery and chemical manufacturers and financiers. This community of interests on the tariff question is not a mere matter of chance, for the financial and personal relationships between landowners, industrialists, and bankers are intimate. The big industrialists, indeed, have profited directly from the wheat campaign by reason of the greatly expanded domestic market for machinery and chemical fertilizers.[44]

[43] Rivera, *Il problema agronomico nel Mezzogiorno d'Italia*, p. 27.

[44] The declared profits of the great chemical firm, Montecatini—which has a virtual monopoly in the production of artificial fertilizers in Italy—rose from 47,000,000 lire in 1924 to 64,000,000 in 1925, 101,000,000 in 1926, 103,000,000 in 1937, and averaged 77,000,000 per year during 1928-33. Its capitalization throughout the period 1925-33 was 500,000,000 lire. Associazione fra le Società Italiane per Azione, *Notizie Statistiche*, Vols. XII, XIV. In 1934 the capitalization rose to 600,000,000 lire, and in 1936 to 800,000,000 lire. It is precisely the consumption of fertilizers produced largely in Italy—namely nitrates—that has increased to a great extent since 1925; that of imported phosphates and potash salts has risen only slowly. In its business report for 1929, Montecatini points to its concern over the development of Italian agriculture and to its happy associations with the technical directors of the wheat campaign: "Our relations with the traveling chairs of agriculture have been excellent, and we have sought to favor the chairs as much as possible, being fully convinced that, thanks to the work of their directors, the development and technical progress of the nation's

Directly opposed to this alignment of interests are the millions of small peasant farmers, agricultural workers, and industrial workers, whose welfare both as income-earners and consumers would be best served by cheap production goods and cheap food—which would call for abolition of the high duties on industrial products and on wheat.

To strike a balance, it may be said that in consequence of the wheat campaign, domestic output has been raised appreciably, and that Italy's dependence on wheat imports is much reduced. Furthermore, the prestige of the Fascist regime at home and abroad undoubtedly has been enhanced. It is something to be able to point to a concrete and marked advance in the production of wheat, a commodity easy to sentimentalize, especially in Italy. Also, the profits of the landowners and industrialists have been increased. On the other hand, the cost of these achievements has been serious disturbance of the agricultural equilibrium of the nation, possible future reduction in productivity, unnecessary loss of export markets for products more economically produced than wheat, and higher living costs for urban and rural workers.

---

agriculture will be effected more easily than by any other method." Quoted by Vöchting, "Die italienische Getreideschlacht," p. 34. The declared profits of *Fiat*, the leading Italian producer of tractors, also rose appreciably after 1924.

V: Reclaiming the Soil

The integral reclamation of our national territory is an enterprise the achievement of which would alone suffice to make the revolution of the Blackshirts glorious down the centuries.

—MUSSOLINI[1]

FOR centuries the Italian people has struggled against wind and water for possession of the soil. Almost everywhere in Italy the hills and mountains—long ago deforested—are subject to continuous erosion; the sediment-laden streams are forever threatening to form water-damming barriers in the plains. Thus rocky highlands and barren, marshy wastes have developed in many parts of the country.[2] But for generations old fields have been saved from destruction and new lands have been wrested from swamp and steppe by the building of dykes, terraces, drainage canals, and irrigation ditches. The names of emperors, popes, and princes are associated with ambitious land-reclamation projects—some brilliant successes, others dismal failures. Always, however, the unending, patient

[1] Speech to farmers and peasants, Rome, October 14, 1928.

[2] Two great areas, the lower plain of the Po and the central western littoral of the peninsula, have suffered in this way particularly. The building of embankments about the mouths of the Po system tended to block the flow of water into the Adriatic, leading to periodic floods and the development of marshes. Dunes also have interfered with proper drainage in the Tuscan Maremma and the plain of the Tiber; furthermore, here as elsewhere in the South, during the rainy season the water rushes in torrents down the treeless slopes of the coastal hills, inundating the narrow plains and converting parts of them into morasses. Drainage and canalization are not sufficient here; corrective work in the hinterland, including reforestation, is also essential. This is a slow, painful, and often fruitless combat with mountains in geologic disorder, with earthquakes, landslides, and highly irregular watercourses.

labor of the peasant masses has been basic in this work of saving and winning land.

Thus some of the most fertile areas today were reclaimed long before the unification of Italy. But the earlier works generally were restricted in scope and limited in effect. The inception of modern, large-scale, extensive land reclamation must be linked with the rise of capitalistic agriculture in the North. A profound transformation of agriculture, in large part based on the investment of private capital in drainage and irrigation works, accompanied the political and industrial development of North Italy in the first half of the nineteenth century. Already by 1860 the basis of an intensive, commercialized agriculture had been laid in the Po valley. Many of the major tasks of reclamation had been completed and in a number of important areas the only further requirement was maintenance of dykes and canals. In the economically backward South, however, little had been done except in the vicinity of cities.

Although the wealthy landowners associated in consortia were successful in clearing and irrigating much land, the drainage of vast marshy areas—such as those around the mouths of the Po—was beyond their financial means. The government was not slow in providing assistance. Even before 1860, government aid for private drainage schemes was extended in Piedmont, Lombardy, Venetia, and Tuscany. Since the unification the national government has participated in reclamation work on a steadily increasing scale.

After 1900 the sphere of government reclamation activity was broadened by the need to provide employment for the growing army of jobless farm laborers and by recognition of a public responsibility in combating malaria and in improving the physical basis of agriculture in the South. At the same time, the concept of reclamation was changing. Originally, there was little regional or national coördination of the work. Each individual drainage project was looked upon as an entity, and insufficient consideration was given to the possibility that its success might be contingent on simultaneous works in adjacent hilly areas, or on intensive cultivation of the lands once they were drained. Too frequently, the result of this narrow view of the problem meant a wastage of labor and capital. Gradually it was realized that the government must, if drainage works were to be effective, insist on complete reclamation of surrounding regions and be ready to force landowners under threat of expropriation to carry on the necessary subsequent improvement of the land. Comprehension of the intricate economic and technical problems and implications of land salvage showed that reclamation must go beyond drainage and irrigation in the plains to control of torrents and reforestation in the mountains, and finally also to provision of roads, drinking water, barns, stables, and even a cultivating population in the reclaimed districts. The term *bonifica integrale* ("integral land reclamation"), connoting *all* the works necessary to transformation of an uncultivated or inefficiently cultivated region into intensively farmed land, thus gained currency.

These tendencies toward greater state initiative and authority and toward wider scope of the works are reflected in the development of the legislative basis of reclamation. As early as 1865 the national government provided for flood control through construction of dykes and regulation of river courses at public expense. In 1873 a law pertaining to the reclamation of the Agro Romano authorized expropriation of recalcitrant landowners. But Italy's modern reclamation legislation begins with the "Baccarini Law" of 1882, which laid down important guiding lines for all subsequent legislation. It provided for state execution of more important works on some 800,000 hectares, three-fourths of the costs to be borne by the national and communal governments and one-fourth by the landowners. The government's task was to end with drainage; any further work necessary was to be undertaken by the landowners alone. Between 1882 and the World War numerous legislative actions gradually broadened the field of state activity and the nature of the works to be undertaken. Thus, a law of 1883 called for improvement of drained lands in the Agro Romano, under pain of expropriation; one of 1900, authorizing expenditure of 250,000,000 lire for reclamation in the South, conceived of the works as including road building, prevention of landslides, and reforestation; others in 1912 included among the objects of reclamation the supply of drinking water and made obligatory on proprietors the further improvement of reclaimed land.[3] In 1911 a special committee representing the Ministries of Public Works and Commerce, Industry and Agriculture was established in order to prepare a coördinated national plan for reclamation, reforestation, and regulation of streams.[4] By 1912 all major elements of the recent Fascist reclamation program had been conceived.

Actual achievements in reclamation work before the Fascist era, while not so extensive as contemplated by the legislative

[3] See Buccella, "Lo svolgimento ed il sistema della bonifica integrale," pp. 587 ff.; Vöchting, *Die Urbarmachung der römischen Campagna*, pp. 521-27.

[4] In the years immediately after the World War there were numerous legislative proposals that were intended to broaden the social character of reclamation. Most important was a bill adopted by the Chamber of Deputies in 1922 which would have provided for large reclamation subsidies by the government, expropriation of landowners in favor of the coöperative societies of peasants, and execution of the projects by these coöperatives. This bill was withdrawn by the Fascist government a few weeks after the "March on Rome."

appropriations, were considerable—certainly much more important than recent Italian commentators are willing to admit. In 1911 a leading agricultural economist stated that during the period 1862-1911 the national and local governments had spent 240,000,000 lire for reclamation purposes, and that 550,000 hectares had been drained.[5] The Fascist Minister of Finance in 1924 estimated that during 1860-1924 expenditures of 1,162,000,000 lire had been authorized, that 666,000,000 had actually been spent, and that by the end of 1922, 597,000 hectares had been drained (of which 324,000 were already under cultivation), and that reclamation works were then progressing on 623,000 hectares.[6] Results in terms of public health and agricultural productivity were noteworthy. From the decade 1882-91 to that of 1912-21 the average malaria death rate in North Italy fell 86 per cent, and the population

[5] Valenti, "L'Italia agricola dal 1861 al 1911," p. 117.

[6] De' Stefani, *L'azione dello Stato Italiano per le opere pubbliche, 1862-1924*, p. 120.

The reclamation outlays fluctuated considerably from year to year, varying largely with the state of the public finances. However, there was a marked upward trend throughout the period after 1862. Thus, actual expenditures in various pre-War years are estimated to have been: *1870*, 500,000 lire; *1880*, 12,000,000; in the fiscal year *1890-91*, 7,000,000; *1903-4*, 10,000,000; *1914-15*, 20,000,000. Buccella, *op. cit.*, p. 596. Post-War outlays, in gold lire per fiscal year, were: *1918-19*, 65,000,000; *1919-20*, 50,000,000; *1920-21*, 76,000,000; *1921-22*, 50,000,000. Ministero delle Finanze, *Il bilancio dello Stato dal 1913-14 al 1929-30*, p. 370.

These estimates refer to major reclamation projects. Another investigator places the total area of uncultivable land in Italy in 1882 at 3,700,000 hectares, of which area 2,100,000 hectares had been reclaimed by the end of 1922. Ucker, *Die italienische Agrarpolitik seit 1925*, p. 26. For another estimate, see Salvemini, "Can Italy Live at Home?", pp. 252-53. The variety of works comprised under the general term "reclamation," as well as the broadening of the concept itself, make difficult strict comparison of the achievements in various periods.

It should be noted that little was accomplished before the War in the field of reforestation: during 1867-1910 only 34,000 hectares were reforested by the State. Valenti, *op. cit.*, p. 117.

and number of farm animals in the reclaimed zones increased by 64 and 134 per cent, respectively. It is also estimated that, as a result of reclamation, the value of agricultural production in the North was increased between these two periods by 900,000,000 lire a year.[7]

The northern provinces were the chief beneficiaries of the pre-War reclamation work. Much good will was shown toward the South in appropriations and in actual expenditures,[8] but little headway was made because of failure to reduce the torrential character of the mountain streams, the resistance and inertia of absentee proprietors, and the persistence of malaria even after land had been brought under more intensive cultivation.[9]

The methods and results of land reclamation in the half-century before the Fascist regime thus cannot be characterized as ill-conceived or insignificant. Indeed, viewed historically, the Fascist reclamation policy is but an extension of pre-War tendencies. Legislation and administration in recent years have reflected the trend toward a widening concept of the problem and increasing government intervention that had begun well before the War.[10] Moreover, as in earlier times, the degree of

[7] Buccella, *op. cit.*, p. 597.

[8] Reclamation expenditures in the South during the period 1862-1924 were equal to those in North and Central Italy. De' Stefani (*op. cit.*, p. 131) estimates the total outlays by regions, in millions of lire, in the period 1862-1924 as follows: North Italy, 94.6; Central Italy, 231.4; South Italy, 325.6.

[9] It is now believed by some malariologists that the malarial mosquito of the South is of a race distinct from that of the North. The southern Anopheles shows a distinct preference for human hosts, whereas her northern relative prefers other animals. Thus, the introduction of intensive cultivation and farm animals is not enough to stop malaria in the South, although it is in the North.

[10] In their more considered statements, the Fascist reclamation experts admit this. But the ardent propagandists imply that, at least in Italy, land reclamation is exclusively a Fascist invention.

governmental activity has been markedly influenced by the financial exigencies of the landowners, the extent of unemployment, and the condition of the public finances. Measured in terms of financial and physical magnitude, however, the Fascist reclamation program is undeniably impressive.

ORGANIZATION AND METHODS

For four or five years after the "March on Rome" the Fascist Government showed little concern for reclamation—less, indeed, than its immediate predecessors. To be sure, laws that broadened the field of state activity and provided for more thorough execution of reclamation works were enacted in 1923 and 1924.

A law of December 30, 1923, made a distinction between reclamation projects with a substantial "social interest" (which were to be carried out, directly or indirectly, by the government) and minor projects (to be undertaken by private enterprise with governmental assistance). The so-called Lex Serpieri of May 18, 1924, widened the field still further. "In addition to the redemption, from the economic and hygienic standpoint, of the marshy areas only, the object of this law is to secure the intensification of production in those regions where waste lands exist, whatever may be the cause . . . of such conditions." Thus, there would be classified as "districts of agricultural transformation" all areas in which agriculture is in a backward condition, but which appear capable of improvement.[11] This law also provided that the work would generally be undertaken by State-supported consortia of landowners, which might be formed under compulsion. Obstreperous landowners might be expropriated in favor of such consortia, or, if this were not likely to be effective, in favor of private joint-stock

[11] Costanzo, "The General Scheme of Land Improvement in Italy," p. 168.

companies or private capitalists who would agree to carry out the necessary work. This law is similar to the bill withdrawn by the Fascists in 1922, except that it allows expropriation by capitalistic enterprise, and makes no provision for expropriation in favor of peasants' societies.

But this legislation had little financial support, for the government was concerned with effecting budgetary economies, and unemployment was not a serious problem. For several years, in fact, government outlays for reclamation declined. Expenditures by fiscal years were as follows (in millions of gold lire): *1922-23*, 45; *1923-24*, 26; *1924-25*, 40; *1925-26*, 33; *1926-27*, 55.[12] Work was largely limited to maintenance and continuation of projects already begun. For example, 172 projects were in course of execution on June 30, 1926; of this number, 132 had been begun before October 28, 1922, and 36 before 1900; only 38,000 hectares were affected by the works started after October 28, 1922.[13]

With the onset of agricultural depression—and all that it meant in financial strain on agriculturists and unemployment of rural workers—the government began to take interest in a large-scale reclamation program. Mussolini sounded the call for this new activity in October 1926, when he declared: "It is our task to change beyond all recognition the physical and spiritual face of our country within the space of ten years." During 1927 official and unofficial announcements were made of a vast, "integrated" program, that eventually would give new land to millions of Italian peasants. The "Mussolini Law" of December 24, 1928, authorized a financial plan for the ambitious program: a total of 7,000,000,000 lire was to

[12] Ministero delle Finanze, *Il bilancio dello Stato dal 1913-14 al 1929-30*, p. 370. The cost of drainage was rising throughout this period; therefore, even less was accomplished than these figures suggest.

[13] Ministero dei Lavori Pubblici, *Le opere pubbliche*, pp. 212 ff.

be expended over a period of 14 years, 4,350,000,000 to be advanced by the government and 2,650,000,000 by the landowners. It also fixed the proportions of governmental and private expenditures for various classes of projects, extended the scope of reclamation to include all work necessary to initiate intensive cultivation, and coördinated older reclamation laws and regulations. Late in 1929 an Undersecretariat for Land Reclamation was set up in the Ministry of Agriculture, for general administration of the program. More recent laws have modified the financial scope and technical processes envisaged by the Mussolini Law. The basic pattern has, however, remained essentially the same.[14]

The legal framework of the program is, briefly, as follows. All works are classified, on the basis of their presumed social importance, as (1) "land-reclamation" works, and (2) "land-improvement" works. The former, which are expected to be of broad public significance in terms of production, hygiene, and colonization, are to be carried out largely at government expense, with compulsory contributions by landowners, in legally delimited districts under a general, coördinated plan. On the other hand, land-improvement works are to be executed voluntarily by the owners, supported by government subsidies, primarily for the benefit of one or more farms and independently of any general reclamation plan.[15] It is intended

[14] For texts of the more important laws see International Institute of Agriculture, *Annuaire internationale de législation agricole, 1923, 1924, 1928, 1929, 1933.* Summary descriptions are to be found in: International Institute of Agriculture, *Monthly Bulletin of Agricultural Economics and Sociology,* April 1929, pp. 167-72; May 1935, pp. 161-74; Longobardi, *Land Reclamation in Italy.*

[15] For works of the first class, the government's share ranges as high as 84 per cent of the total outlay in North and Central Italy, excepting the Julian Venetia, the Tuscan Maremma and Latium, and up to 92 per cent in these latter regions and in the South and the Islands. The entire cost of moun-

that the expenditures of the landowners will be remunerative in terms of increased income from the reclaimed lands. Furthermore, two main types of reclamation works are recognized: (1) those directed toward *converting* thinly populated and extensively or little cultivated areas into regions of intensive farming ("transformative" works), and (2) those intended to help in *maintaining* efficient cultivation in more advanced farming areas ("protective" works).

The territory to be reclaimed is divided into districts, and the landowners in each district are called upon to organize a consortium. The consortia are the basic executive agencies in the program: they plan the work, act as coördinators between proprietors, government, and credit institutions for financing purposes, and often directly undertake the necessary works.[16] A consortium may be formed either voluntarily by the individuals owning a major portion of the land in a particular district, or under government compulsion. Its management is chosen by the owners concerned, and its activities are subject to supervision by the Undersecretariat. The decisions of a consortium are binding upon all landowners of the district. Thus, in order to oblige owners to shoulder the burden of reclamation, a consortium may initiate a project, for which all landowners become at once financially responsible. If a proprietor is unable or unwilling to assume such responsibility, he may be expropriated by the consortium, the expropriation indemnity being the capital value of the land's net income. All consortia must become members of the National Associa-

---

tain works, reforestation, and regulation of streams is borne by the government. For "land-improvement" works, the subsidy to the landowner is generally a third of the total cost.

[16] The government itself may directly plan and execute a particular project. Also, the Serpieri law of 1924 empowered joint-stock companies to undertake reclamation work and to expropriate inactive landowners.

tion of Reclamation Consortia, which exercises general supervisory functions and provides its members with technical and financial assistance. The central coördinating organ is the Undersecretariat for Land Reclamation.[17]

Only a small part of the financial burden entailed by the program falls immediately on the government and landowners. The government's share is paid largely in instalments over a period of thirty years, and the landowners' obligations also take the form of annual payments, covering both the capital value of their burden and the interest thereon. The consortia thus receive claims against the government and owners, on the security of which they borrow the necessary funds from various credit institutions, notably the savings banks and the social-insurance organizations. A committee representing the leading credit agencies and the National Association of Consortia supervises these discount operations.

Work of "mountain improvement"—mainly reforestation and regulation of mountain streams—has also been integrated into the general reclamation scheme and is undertaken entirely by the government.

The fundamental "guiding principles" of the governmental aspects of the program are outlined by the Undersecretariat for Land Reclamation as follows:

The State, by its intervention in regard to private works of land improvement, has no intention of substituting its own will and its own judgment for the will and judgment of the individual landowners, but only to ensure that the landowners, while act-

[17] Other governmental agencies concerned with various aspects of the program are the Forest Militia, the Civil Engineering Corps, the Agricultural Inspectorate, the Public Health Service, and the Commissariat for Internal Migration. The National Secretariat for Mountains and the National Society of War Veterans—two "semi-public" organizations—also have special reclamation functions.

ing according to their own advantage, as they themselves deem it, shall act within such limits and under such rules as are recognized to be necessary for the attainment of the "public objects" of reclamation and improvement.

All schemes must make the territory in question healthful, increase farm production and employment of labor, assure to the working population the possibility of living a "rural life," and afford employment to permanent workers bound to the soil as small independent farmers, tenants, or share-croppers.[18]

RECLAMATION IN PRACTICE

Extraordinary difficulties are met with in any attempt to evaluate fairly the practical significance of the Fascist reclamation program. The sources of information contain many pitfalls of vague concepts, contradictory data, extravagant claims; all too often information is non-existent. A high degree of caution and skepticism obviously is necessary.[19]

Of course the concept of reclamation itself is a source of trouble. Its meaning in Italy has gradually been stretched far beyond drainage and irrigation works to include almost *any* work that may permit more intensive cultivation of a given

[18] See Costanzo, "Comprehensive Reclamation and Land Improvement in Italy," pp. 167-68.

[19] The chief sources of data are two censuses of public works (1926 and 1929), a census of reclamation projects (1930), various publications of the Federazione Nazionale delle Bonifiche (1923-27), and publications of the Undersecretariat for Land Reclamation (1931-35). These documents are prime examples of the use of quantitative data for politically convenient under- and overstatement. The officials frequently argue (and with some reason) that, in any absolute sense, a reclamation project never ends, and that, furthermore, it is as yet too early to evaluate properly the results of work begun in recent years. But this does not excuse confusion and obscurity with respect to the status of the various projects under way at a given moment.

area. Thus, in order fairly to compare the "reclamation" outlays in one period with those in another, precise distinction between the types of works undertaken in the two periods is necessary. But such distinction can be made only with extreme difficulty on the basis of the official information.

Unfortunately, most Italian scholars and experts are unable or unwilling to undertake to bring some order out of this chaos of information. The many unofficial Italian studies of reclamation uncritically mirror the official version, and frequently pile exaggeration on exaggeration in the effort to compliment the Fascist regime and to detract from the work of earlier governments. The purpose of most of these studies obviously is political flattery, not serious inquiry. Salvemini quotes a writer in *Lavoro* (September 1, 1931) as declaring: "Seldom or never has it been possible to ascertain, even from specialists, in any precise and positive manner, what has actually been done and what is still being done for this great problem."[20]

As observed before, expenditures for reclamation declined for several years after inauguration of the Fascist regime. The annual average governmental outlays (in terms of gold lire) were 17 per cent less during the fiscal years 1922-27 than during 1918-22.[21] Only in the year 1927-28 did expenditures begin to rise appreciably.

Taken at their face value, the data in Table 4 indicate an enormous increase in reclamation activity since 1927.[22] Accord-

[20] "Land Reclamation and Fascism."

[21] Ministero delle Finanze, *Il bilancio dello Stato dal 1913-14 al 1929-30*, p. 370.

[22] However, the reclamation outlays have been small in comparison with other government expenditures. Army and navy outlays in the financial years 1922-34 were more than seven times as great as those for reclamation. In one fiscal year, 1933-34, the outlays for military and police purposes were greater than those for reclamation in the five years after the enactment of the "Mussolini Law," 1929-34. Istituto Centrale di Statistica, *Annuario*

TABLE 4

PUBLIC AND PRIVATE EXPENDITURES FOR RECLAMATION[23]

1870-1936

In millions of lire: 1927-36 gold value

FISCAL YEARS	GOVERNMENT WORKS		PRIVATE WORKS	TOTAL
	Reclamation and trans-formation	*Mountain improve-ment*		
1870–1922	1,720.5	62.2		1,782.7
1922–1923	210.7	18.1	14.7	243.5
1923–1924	141.00	12.7	36.3	190.0
1924–1925	134.2	10.6	20.0	164.8
1925–1926	178.0	9.1	48.3	255.4
1926–1927	181.8	18.1	88.0	287.9
1927–1928	258.7	30.9	106.5	396.1
1928–1929	341.0	39.8	130.4	511.2
1929–1930	617.1	42.8	255.7	915.6
1930–1931	465.2	34.5	248.5	748.2
1931–1932	495.1	34.9	207.8	737.8
1932–1933	505.0	49.4	285.7	840.1
1933–1934	543.4	47.7	282.9	874.0
1934–1935	615.9	56.2	358.1	1,030.2
1935–1936	490.2	37.7	283.8	811.7

ing to official claims, the total authorized expenditures from 1870 to July 1, 1935 were 11,768,700,000 lire and the cost of the works actually executed in this period was 9,769,200,000. Of these amounts, 8,697,100,000 and 7,986,500,000, respectively, pertain to the Fascist era.[24]

The total of 4,115,700,000 lire expended during the five

Statistico, 1935, p. 209. The greatly increased military expenditures since 1934 must make State support of reclamation schemes increasingly difficult.

[23] Data for 1870-1934 from Serpieri, *La legge sulla bonifica integrale nel quinto anno di applicazione*, p. 81; data for 1934-1936 from the Istituto Centrale di Statistica. It is to be noted that the great bulk of the expenditures before 1922 was concentrated in the years 1904-14 and 1919-22.

[24] Data from the Istituto Centrale di Statistica.

years 1929-30 to 1933-34 was distributed as follows (in millions of lire):[25]

A. *Government Projects*	
1. Drainage works, related defensive works (such as road making, irrigation works, mountain improvement), and land improvement in the public interest	2,618.0
2. Roads in connection with land improvement	7.8
3. Mountain improvement	209.3
B. *Private Projects with Government Subsidy*	
1. Irrigation and search for water	567.7
2. Rural aqueducts	101.8
3. Farm roads	40.4
4. Rural buildings	122.0
5. Breaking of land	25.0
6. Minor land improvements	144.6
7. Private works on the Roman Campagna and Agro Pontino	210.0
8. Provision of drinking water	2.8
9. Improvement of mountain pastures	61.1
10. Provision of electric power for agricultural purposes	5.2

But within the last three years there have been a marked reduction in new works undertaken, a tendency to abandon all projects not urgently needed, and a growing concentration on particular projects that promise to yield immediate political returns.[26] Moreover, total outlays have been drastically reduced since the middle of 1935 (that is, since the initiation of the "imperial phase" of Fascism).[27]

[25] Serpieri, *La legge . . . nel quinto anno*, p. 79.

[26] The amounts authorized for new works have been (in millions of lire): *1929-30*, 244; *1930-31*, 74; *1931-32*, 112.5; *1932-33*, 37.5; *1933-34*, 17.8. *Ibid.*, p. 83.

[27] The total number of man-days of work on public reclamation projects fell from 22,145,082 in 1934 to 16,007,380 in 1935, and to 10,240,928

The physical extent of reclamation work in recent years seems at first sight even more impressive than the financial outlays. On July 1, 1934, the total area of reclamation districts was 8,181,000 hectares and that of "mountain systematization" districts was 6,556,000 hectares.[28] Thus, nearly *half* of the total area of Italy officially was subject to reclamation works of one kind or another. But these area data refer to districts in which a variety of works (comprehended under the present broad concept of "integral reclamation") are actually under way *or* merely projected *or* considered desirable. One need only scan the lists of individual districts in order to recognize the illusory character of much of the data.[29] In many districts, "reclamation" is a distant and vague hope rather than an actuality. It is necessary, therefore, to turn to data on reclamation projects actually completed or in course of execution.

On July 1, 1934, reclamation works had been "completed"

in 1936. Istituto Centrale di Statistica, *Annuario Statistico, 1936*, p. 149; *1937*, p. 173. Franco Angelini, president of the Agricultural-Workers' Confederation, admitted in May 1937, that "reclamation is marking time for reasons of a contingent nature. But it is hoped that the work can soon be got under way again." *Lavoro Fascista*, May 15, 1937.

[28] Serpieri, *La legge . . . nel quinto anno*, p. 422.

[29] For instance, 330,000 hectares in Istria are said to be under reclamation. But "reclamation" in this case consists solely of construction of an aqueduct for supplying drinking water to towns and villages, of reforestation of 50,000 hectares of communal lands, and of drainage of a few hundred hectares. Work has been "completed" on only 10,000 hectares, and is "not far advanced" on the remaining 320,000 hectares. Similar instances are to be found in other parts of the country. It is interesting to note that the great increase in the area of reclamation districts, 1932-33, was largely the result of an extension of the term "reclamation" to include works of "transformation" and road building. Obviously, when the term "reclamation" can connote even the construction of barns, stables, drinking troughs, and roads, it is quite possible that as much as 70 per cent of such an advanced agricultural region as Emilia should be included within "reclamation districts."

or were "under way" on some 4,734,000 hectares, that is, on almost *one-sixth* of the total area of the country. The extent of the various classes of works on this area was (in thousands of hectares):[30]

1. "Protective" works		
a. "Fully or nearly completed"	979.9	
b. "In course of execution but not far advanced"	1,046.2	2,026.1
2. "Transformative" works		
a. Preliminary works "fully or nearly completed" and transformation "well advanced or completed" ...	782.6	
b. Preliminary works "fully or nearly completed" but transformation "not yet begun"	330.2	
c. Preliminary works "in course of execution but not far advanced" ..	1,595.1	2,707.9

At first glance, an amazingly large part of the country would seem to be under *actual* reclamation. But these data, too, are very misleading. For one thing, 43 per cent (2,026,100 hectares) of the total area of 4,734,000 hectares is land on which there is already more or less intensive cultivation. On such land, "reclamation" consists simply of maintenance of drainage canals, irrigation ditches, dykes, etc.—most of which have been in existence for decades. Secondly, more than half (51.7 per cent of the areas under "protective reclamation" and 58.8 per cent of those under transformative reclamation") of the total area has been scarcely touched. The works "in course of execution but not far advanced" in most instances exist only

[30] Serpieri, *La legge . . . nel quinto anno*, p. 93. On July 1, 1936, the total area in reclamation districts had grown 8,718,934 hectares, and the area in which works were "completed" or "under way" was 5,106,938 hectares. Istituto Centrale di Statistica, *Annuario Statistico, 1937*, p. 63. Data on the nature and progress of works in this area are not available.

on paper—that is, only the preliminary surveys, estimates and plans have been completed. Thirdly, the group of "fully completed" works includes many that were already completed or in an advanced stage by October 28, 1922.[31] Finally, the term "nearly completed" often means that very much remains to be done before the work can be considered fully executed.[32]

Substantial progress, therefore, had been made on less than half (2,090,700 hectares) of the total area on which reclamation works were officially declared (on July 1, 1934) to be completed or under way.[33] The largest territory under rec-

[31] Thus, the official reports include the Sarnese and Nocerino districts (near Naples), which were reclaimed about fifty years ago, among the "completed" areas.

[32] Unfortunately, the official reports give only inferential information on the amount of work necessary to complete projects that are under way, merely projected, or still in the realm of fancy. For example, on page 384 of Serpieri's 1934 report the works on 34,260 hectares in the Padano-Polesano district are listed as "fully or nearly completed" on July 1, 1934, yet on page 10 is the statement that only a year before all these works were merely "under way," and that slightly over a million lire had been expended upon them. Obviously, such projects have gone little beyond the preliminary stage of plans and surveys.

Public discussions sometimes lead, perhaps unwittingly, to deflation of official claims. For instance, in the course of a meeting of reclamation experts in 1934 a certain engineer, Ramadoro, pointed out that according to official declarations some 26,000 hectares in Apulia had been "reclaimed," but that actually only 6,000 hectares had benefited from the building of canals and roads, and that the remaining 20,000 hectares were still in the same condition as formerly. R. Accademia dei Georgofili, "Convegno per la bonifica integrale," pp. 327-28.

[33] The physical extent of the major works *completed* in the period July 1, 1922-December 31, 1931 is estimated as follows:

1. Drainage canals	12,197	kilometers
2. Dykes and embankments	3,644	kilometers
3. Lands filled	322,101	cubic meters
4. Complementary roads	5,867	kilometers
5. Bridges (number)	16,320	
6. Area drained	661,901	hectares
7. Principal irrigation canals	1,434	kilometers

lamation is the lower Po basin, an area of about a million hectares. Here the bulk of the first work of drainage and irrigation had been completed before the World War. The major regions in peninsular Italy are those of the alluvial plains adjacent to the Tyrrhenian Sea, from the Serchio to the Sela, notably the Tuscan Maremma, the lands beside the mouth of the Tiber, the Roman Campagna, the Agro Pontino, and the Neapolitan Campania. In all these areas, where drainage is the principal task, considerable advances appear to have been made in recent years. Accomplishments have been much more modest in the heel and toe of the peninsula and in Sicily, where irrigation, colonization, transformation of the *latifondi*, and reforestation—rather than drainage—are most essential.

Similar observations must be made in respect of the mountain area of 6,556,000 hectares (74.7 per cent of the total mountain area of the country) which on July 1, 1934 was officially the object of "mountain systematization." It would be more accurate to say that three-fourths of Italy's mountain lands were desperately in need of repair of the damages resulting from deforestation and erosion, rather than to imply that repairs on such a scale actually have been undertaken. Although the works desirable for this purpose would be enormous, the amounts expended and the accomplishments have been relatively slight.[34]

---

8. Area made irrigable .... 201,592 hectares
9. Aqueducts .... 837 kilometers

Serpieri, *La legge . . . nel quinto anno*, pp. 84-86. There is no indication, however, of the period during which these works had been under way.

[34] During the five fiscal years 1929-34, 209,300,000 lire were spent for "mountain systematization." Hydraulic and forest systematization had been "completed" on 124,367 hectares and were "in course of execution" on 168,345 hectares; 46,431 hectares had been reforested. *Ibid.*, pp. 75-79, 463; Istituto Centrale di Statistica, *Annuario Statistico, 1935*, p. 64.

The exaggeration implicit in the official summary data is especially marked in respect of the works "under way" in Central and Southern Italy. The following table shows, in percentages, the extent of "protective" and "transformative" reclamation works in the major regions of the country and their state of development on July 1, 1934:[35]

	North	*Center*	*South and Islands*
"Protective" works	71.6	14.6	23.2
"Transformative" works	28.4	85.4	76.8
	100.0	100.0	100.0
"Protective" works			
a. "Fully or nearly completed"	33.3	6.7	12.6
b. "In course of execution, not far advanced"	38.3	7.9	10.6
"Transformative" works			
a. Preliminary works "fully or nearly completed"	25.6	7.3	26.8
b. Preliminary works "in course of execution but not far advanced	2.8	78.1	50.0
	100.0	100.0	100.0

Obviously, in the North considerable progress has been made toward completion of the projected works, but in the remainder of the country the bulk of the work is still in a preliminary stage.

Furthermore, there has been an extraordinary concentration of work in one relatively small area, the Agro Pontino. This region of about 75,000 hectares of marsh and dunes,

[35] Based on data in Serpieri, *op. cit.*, p. 93.

within 60 kilometers of Rome, offered the Fascist regime an opportunity to carry out a project of great demonstrative value. The Pontino, for centuries malaria-ridden, scantily populated, and of little use other than as poor pasture for half-wild cattle, had been the object of repeated unsuccessful attempts at reclamation.[36] Its conversion, regardless of cost, into a region of small farms intensively cultivated by war-veteran colonists must become—with appropriate publicity—an important source of prestige for the regime.

A consortium of landowners began reclamation work in the Pontino on May 20, 1922. Little progress, however, was made for some years; by July 1, 1926, the total expenditures had been only 20,000,000 lire.[37] It was then decided to convert the project into a demonstration of Fascist enterprise and power. The major tasks of reclamation and colonization were turned over to the *Opera Nazionale Combattenti* (the National Society of War Veterans), the government's propaganda machinery was directed toward advertising the scheme, and public funds were poured lavishly and at an increasing rate into the venture. By March 1, 1936, not less than 1,000,000,000 lire had been expended on the Pontino.[38] Nearly a third of all funds, public and private, spent for reclamation, land improvement, and "mountain systematization" throughout the

[36] Although usually styled "the Pontine Marshes," most (roughly 60 per cent) of the region was covered by sand dunes before the recent reclamation.

[37] Federazione Nazionale delle Bonifiche, *Le bonifiche in Italia al 1 luglio 1926*, pp. 34-35.

[38] Information from the Undersecretariat for Land Reclamation. This total does not include outlays for construction of "cities" in the district. The expenditures were 203,000,000 lire in the four fiscal years 1926-32, 223,000,000 in the two fiscal years 1932-34, and 600,000,000 from July 1, 1934 to March 1, 1936. This represents more than one-eighth of the total outlays, public and private, since July 1, 1926, for reclamation, land improvement, and "mountain systematization" throughout the country.

country since July 1, 1932, has been directed to the Pontino.[39]

These expenditures have imposed a heavy burden on the general reclamation program. Other projects, many of which would have had greater social and economic (though less political) significance, have suffered in consequence. The reclamation and transformation of the Roman Campagna, especially, have been held back by reason of the work in the Agro Pontino. The latter offered more impressive possibilities of astonishing the world, because it would be work *ex novo*. So after 1931 the state credits that previously were going into the Campagna reclamation were diverted to the Pontino. Soon it was receiving far more State support than the Campagna ever had.[40]

Moreover, maintenance of the work accomplished in the Pontino will call for further heavy outlays in the future. Some of the land has proved to be poor and unable to support the considerable number of colonists originally intended for it; apparently there is danger, too, that large expenditures will be needed for a long period to prevent the drained areas from turning into arid dunes.[41] Nevertheless, the venture probably

[39] Further evidence of the great concentration of effort on the Pontino is provided by data on employment in public works projects. For instance, in 1934 the number of man-days employed in the Agro Pontino—11,400,000—was 25 per cent of the total in all public works and 63 per cent of the total in all reclamation projects. Longobardi, *Land Reclamation in Italy*, p. 142; Istituto Centrale di Statistica, *Annuario Statistico, 1935*, p. 237.

[40] Vöchting, *Die Urbarmachung*, pp. 535-37.

[41] In a speech at Littoria (capital of the new province established in the Pontino) on December 18, 1932, Mussolini declared that eventually 40,000-50,000 colonists would be settled in the reclaimed region. On August 19, 1936, the Duce announced that the reclamation of the Pontino was completed. At the end of 1935 the number of new colonist families established was 2,215, comprising 19,048 individuals. Nannini, "La migrazione e la colonizzazione," p. 96. However, allowance ought to be made for the peasant families living in the nearby hills who, because of the new settle-

has been satisfactory in terms of publicity for the colonization and reclamation programs of the Fascists. Foreign visitors, in particular, usually are impressed favorably by a hurried trip through the "reclaimed Pontine Ager"—the "Potemkin's villages" of Fascist Italy.

FINANCIAL DIFFICULTIES

As noted above, the Fascist reclamation program envisages large-scale borrowings for works undertaken immediately, and amortization of this debt over a relatively long period. According to the Mussolini Law, the government was pledged to provide 4,350,000,000 lire for projects to be executed within fourteen years; this sum was to be paid largely in annuities over a period of thirty years. But the government was to borrow funds with which to make payments of the annuities; repayment of this debt was to burden the budget up to 1972-73 with annual instalments totaling 9,700,000,000 lire. The landowners were expected to supply another 2,650,000,000 lire, most of which they also would be obliged to borrow. Obviously, in a country so poor in capital as Italy, such financing must reduce the ability of both government and landowners to carry on in the future the necessary works of maintenance and renovation, not to speak of any new works of reclamation that might be desirable.

There is reason to believe that even these large sums authorized for immediate reclamation cannot suffice to complete

ments, have lost such livelihood as they formerly got from the Pontino. The *Opera Nazionale Combattenti* assigns land (10-30 hectares per family), buildings, and live stock to the colonists, who thereupon cultivate the farms as share-tenants. When all necessary advances of money and supplies have been repaid by the head of the colonist family, he may purchase the farm from the *Opera* by making payments over a period of fifteen years. See Longobardi, *op. cit.*, pp. 143-45.

satisfactorily all works that have been initiated. Most regions in Italy where reclamation and reforestation would be highly desirable have been placed within reclamation districts; the inference is that all these regions eventually will be reached by the program. But it has been estimated that at least 24,000,000,000 lire would be necessary for this purpose—that is, more than three times the amount contemplated by the Mussolini Law.[42] Evidently, the necessity of providing work for the growing number of unemployed, of finding fresh fields for capitalistic exploitation, and of meeting the insistent demands for politically spectacular achievements forced the reclamation authorities to go far beyond the limits that would have been imposed in a more permanently effective use of available resources.

Furthermore, a rapid growth in the number of joint-stock companies organized to undertake reclamation works and empowered by law to expropriate inactive proprietors led to a frantic formation of consortia by landowners.[43] Many of these

[42] In 1929 Serpieri held that at least 12,000,000,000 lire would be needed to reclaim the 1,200,000 hectares then already scheduled. Yet by 1935 work of the expensive "transformative" type had been begun on more than twice this area. *Giornale d'Italia*, August 23, 1929. Quoted by Salvemini, "Land Reclamation and Fascism," p. 17. In 1931 Serpieri admitted that "it soon became evident that not the 7,000,000,000 provided by the Mussolini Act, but probably 70,000,000,000 to 80,000,000,000 would be needed to carry out all these works." Serpieri, *La legge sulla bonifica integrale nel primo anno di applicazione*, p. 178. See also David, *La Politique agraire de l'Italie: Les Bonifications*, p. 39.

[43] Some 114 joint-stock reclamation companies were founded in the period 1924-32. Fascist notables were prominent in their organization. Rosenstock-Franck, *L'Économie corporative fasciste*, p. 311. According to the Undersecretariat for Land Reclamation, 1,474 consortia had been organized by July 1, 1935. The fears of expropriation have proved groundless, however. By the end of 1935 only 27,000 hectares—all in the Agro Pontino—had been expropriated because of "failure to meet reclamation obligations." Information from the Undersecretariat for Land Reclamation.

consortia at once began to make plans and obtain approval for reclamation projects, and to borrow money on the security of the promised government subsidies in order to carry out preliminary work (and so escape the danger of expropriation in favor of the joint-stock companies), even when they had little prospect of being able to finance the projects to their completion. The hope that the landowners might secure funds for reclamation by selling a portion of their land has not been realized, partly because of reluctance to sell, partly because of the absence of a substantial demand for land. Hence, in order to provide their share of the expenditures, they have generally been obliged to obtain bank credits.

For various reasons, therefore, projects were begun on a far larger scale than was advisable in terms of the capital limits of the nation in general and of the majority of agriculturists in particular. This has been admitted, at least tacitly, by leading officials. As early as 1931 Arrigo Serpieri (first Undersecretary for Land Reclamation and the leading intellect in the agricultural policy of Fascist Italy) declared, "Too many works have been carried out with insufficient consideration of their economic aspect, resulting in heavy burdens on the land which today are very hard to carry."[44] Later Serpieri pointed out that one of his main concerns as Undersecretary for Land Reclamation was continually to reduce the number of schemes proposed, but that "under the enormous pressure of the [Fascist] workers' representatives" it was impossible to avoid undertaking new projects. Once commitments had been made, the work could not be stopped "without the loss of millions of lire. . . . What we can do practically is to advance more rapidly in certain more adaptable regions, and slow up

[44] Speech at Udine, June 25, 1931, quoted by Salvemini, "Land Reclamation and Fascism," p. 24.

in others, but not to stop."[45] Signor Serpieri might well have added that official approval of new works (and the consequent subsidies) was also often necessary to save large agriculturists and reclamation companies from bankruptcy.

The consequence has been the undertaking of much technically ill-advised work, an enormous growth of agricultural indebtedness, and an extension of the influence of financial institutions over agriculture. In recent years the continual fall of agricultural prices has greatly aggravated the problems of landed indebtedness and has seriously modified the original plans for financing reclamation. The government has been obliged to intervene frequently to rescue debt-burdened landlords.[46] In view of the increasing expenditures for military purposes and of the poverty of the country, it would seem that much of the ambitious reclamation program must eventually be abandoned.

SOCIAL IMPLICATIONS

The Duce has justified the Fascist reclamation program from the social standpoint by declaring that it will "give land and bread to millions of Italians in the future."[47] Following this lead, Fascist commentators place much emphasis on the relief that the *bonifica integrale* will offer to the landless rural population, and on its efficacy as a substitute for emigration to foreign countries. It is suggested, too, that the *latifondi* must now finally be broken up in consequence of sales made necessary by the reclamation program. Widespread publicity has been given to the proposed expropriation of landowners who

[45] R. Accademia dei Georgofili, "Convegno per la bonifica integrale," p. 403.

[46] See below, p. 150.

[47] Speech of October 28, 1928.

"fail in their social duty" to raise the productivity of the land, and this has also been pointed to as a method of reducing the great estates.

In practice, however, the rural masses are given no preferential rights to reclaimed land (with the very limited exception of the war veterans favored by the *Opera Nazionale Combattenti*), although most of the costs of reclamation are borne by the public treasury.[48] Whoever happens to own the land when its increased value is realizable will profit from the government subsidies. The government imposes no obligations with respect to methods of cultivation or employment on the landowners whose property benefits from reclamation.[49] And, as observed above, the Fascist government has been active in assuring continued tenure by the present great landowners. In a speech to the Chamber of Deputies on December 12, 1934, Baron Giacomo Acerbo (then Minister of Agriculture) declared:

> If private property in Italy has resisted all the [recent] tempests . . . this is owing in large measure to the energetic action . . . of the Fascist government. . . . Landed property in Italy has not known the experiments tried in other countries. . . . In fact, while in many countries agrarian reforms—the most benevolent of which meant expropriation of land at half its value—were being carried out . . . and while nearly everywhere private property was bearing the major burdens and suffering the hardest blows of the depression, in Italy, thanks to the action of the Fascist government, private property not only has been saved, but has also been strengthened.[50]

Moreover, the expectation that the big estates would be

[48] Such preference was contemplated in the abortive bill of 1922.

[49] A proposed bill (introduced November 12, 1934) providing for greater pressure on owners to carry out improvement works has so far failed to become law.

[50] Serpieri, *La legge . . . nel quinto anno*, p. 238.

broken up through forced sales or expropriation has proved illusory. Very little land has been sold in order to obtain funds for reclamation. Furthermore, there has been no expropriation for reclamation or transformation purposes except in the Agro Pontino.[51]

The great bulk of Italian farm land is still owned by the aristocracy and the wealthy middle class. Indeed, peasant proprietorship has been declining in recent years; concentration of ownership in relatively few hands is becoming even more pronounced.[52] The financing of the reclamation program itself has been a factor in centralizing control over the land through the medium of the financial institutions and the consortia.

Given the method of constituting the consortia on the basis of majority landownership, it is clear that the larger proprietors and their creditors must be dominant in these organizations. Thus, they are in a position to undertake work that interests them particularly. Only after several years of effort by the Fascist labor-union officials (in the face of strenuous opposition by the landowners) were representatives of local agricultural-workers' unions permitted even to sit on the boards of the consortia. This does not necessarily mean that worker interests are now considered, but probably merely that the union officials can extend their own influence.[53]

[51] The National Society of War Veterans has made but moderate use of its expropriation privileges. Some 105,000 hectares were transferred to the Society in the period 1919-36; of this, it acquired 64,000 by expropriation and the remainder by purchase and donation. Information from the Undersecretariat of Land Reclamation.

[52] See below, pp. 132 ff.

[53] Certain of the "left-wing" Fascist union leaders have been most bitter in their criticism of the administration of the consortia by the landowners. The suggestion has been made that, inasmuch as the proprietors have shown themselves too frequently incapable or unwilling to push ahead rapidly

It is not even certain that the reclamation program will make possible any significant settlement of landless farm workers, even as share-tenants or share-croppers. So far, at least, colonization of internal zones has been a slow process: 8,857 families (comprising 70,367 individuals) were thus settled in the six years ending in October 1936. By the end of 1935, 2,215 of these families were established in the Agro Pontino; it is difficult to estimate how many of the others migrated to newly reclaimed lands.[54] At any rate, in terms of the total number of landless workers, settlement has been exceedingly slight.[55]

Nor must the unfavorable repercussions of reclamation on the mountain peasantry be overlooked. Reforestation and the effort to save existing woods from destruction by cattle have taken pasture lands from many shepherds, and certain of the

---

with reclamation, the expropriation powers ought to be applied. Thus, Franco Angelini (leader of the Agricultural-Workers' Confederation) declared in 1934: "Until yesterday the consortia have been instruments—I speak the truth—in the hands of the big proprietors." R. Accademia dei Georgofili, "Convegno per la bonifica integrale," p. 425. "No longer must the consortium be the exclusive representative of four or twenty or a hundred big proprietors. They must be organs . . . with representatives of laborers as well." Camera dei Deputati, Sessione 1934-1935, *Atti*, Vol. I. And another syndicalist spokesman, replying to Serpieri, insisted: "Yes, sir, the consortia are organs of public law, but they are always subject to extremely personal formulae and viewpoints, and in consequence . . . do not always follow the course necessary in the social interest. . . . I know that there are consortia in Venetia, many of which must be stimulated by the syndical authorities in order to complete work projected in 1916 and not yet finished." R. Accademia dei Georgofili, "Convegno per la bonifica integrale," pp. 345 ff.

[54] Commissariato per le Migrazioni e la Colonizzazione Interne, *Le migrazioni interne, 1934*, p. cii; Ministry of Corporations, *News Notes*, October 1936; Nannini, "La migrazione e la colonizzazione."

[55] The total number of landless farm wageworkers' families in 1931 was 1,360,036. Istituto Centrale di Statistica, *Censimento generale della popolazione . . . 21 aprile, 1931*, Vol. IV, Part 2.

reclamation works in the plains have also had this effect.[56] The Fascist wheat and taxation programs, too, by tending to depress the sheep and goat population, have brought great distress to the highland communities. For these and other reasons, there has been an increasingly pronounced tendency in recent years toward depopulation of the mountain regions.

> It is no longer a question of slow migration from congested mountain communities toward a more promising life in the plains, but rather a rapid transformation of *mezzadri* and little proprietors into day laborers, abandonment of still productive lands, litigation with proprietors concerning debts, or with other members of the tenant family regarding the division of the miserable family income. . . . The migrants tend to increase the number of unemployed *braccianti* of the Po Valley.[57]

Nevertheless, Fascist panegyrists continue to sing:

> Life in the mountain areas pre-eminently demonstrates rural virtues such as attachment to the family and religion; endurance of discomforts; sobriety, discipline, and stability. It has been well said that the sum total of life in the mountains is "the combined prodigy of a mass of privations and sacrifices compensated by satisfactions which are wholly psychological."[58]

Thus, while the Fascist policies have made possible a small amount of new rural settlement, they have at the same time destroyed the source of living for many peasants.

[56] For example, the agricultural economy of the Abruzzi formerly was intimately tied to that of the Roman Campagna. The mountain peasants would bring their sheep into the Campagna for the winter and take them back into the hills in the summer. The extension of crop cultivation in the Campagna, a consequence of reclamation, has greatly reduced its use for sheep pasture. In 1931 the number of sheep in the Campagna was 60 per cent less than in 1926. See Vöchting, *Die Urbarmachung*, p. 466.

[57] Bandino, "Il problema della montagna."

[58] Baravelli, *Integral Land Reclamation in Italy*, p. 19.

The pressure of mounting unemployment after 1927 apparently was an important factor in the wide extension of the reclamation program. Certainly, the *bonifica integrale* has had significance as an unemployment relief program: approximately 30 per cent of all workers employed in public works in the period 1931-35 have been engaged in reclamation schemes.[59] However, this represents, at any one time during the period, not more than 6 per cent of the total unemployment.

The reclamation program has served hygienic ends, particularly in reducing the breeding places of malarial mosquitoes.[60] On the other hand, it has contributed very little toward improvement of rural housing. Despite the shocking conditions in which millions of peasants and farm workers live, subsidies for rural housing totaled only 285,000,000 lire in the fiscal years 1929-35.[61]

The *bonifica integrale*, then, has socially quite a different character from that generally ascribed to it. It is true that land reclamation, irrigation, and reforestation are urgently needed in order to raise the agricultural productivity of Italy, and thereby to provide a means of improving the living levels of the Italian masses. But a system of reclamation essentially subordinated to the exigencies of absentee landed proprietorship concentrating under the controls of monopolistic finance, and limited by the requirements of imperialistic adventure, can have only limited concern for the general welfare. At best, moreover, land improvement can be only a partial solution of

[59] Istituto Centrale di Statistica, *Annuario Statistico, 1935*, p. 237; *1936*, p. 149.

[60] See below, pp. 169-70.

[61] That is, about 5 per cent of total expenditures for reclamation in this period. Information from the Undersecretariat for Land Reclamation. See below, pp. 165-69, for data on rural housing conditions.

the old problem of backward techniques, low production, and consequent poverty. The welfare of the rural masses also demands removal of the tariff barriers erected in the interests of industrial and landed property, a complete reorganization of the systems of land tenure and taxation, and opportunity for emigration.

VI: Landless Farm Workers

At a given moment the worker, the tiller of the soil, must be able to say to himself and to his family: "If I am really better off today it is due to the institutions that the Fascist Revolution has created."

—MUSSOLINI[1]

THE essentials of Fascist labor legislation have been abundantly described; here they will be referred to only briefly.[2] Parallel organizations of workers and employers—the former, at any rate, completely under the control of the government—are established in every branch of the economy. Only one organization in any occupational group is "legally" recognized; in practice all other workers' organizations are prohibited. The parallel "syndicates" conclude labor contracts that bind all employers and workers (members and non-members) of the branch concerned. Again, this is equivalent to saying that the terms of employment are defined by the government hierarchy. All forms of independent criticism on the part of workers—for instance, the strike—are illegal. Disputes involving collective agreements are settled, if possible, through mediation by syndicate officials or the Ministry of Corporations, or by special sessions of the courts—that is, in any case by the government. Mussolini has declared: "The Fascist unions form a great mass completely under the control of Fascism and the government: *a mass that obeys*."[3] No extraordinary

[1] Speech to the National Council of Corporations, November 14, 1933.

[2] For critical accounts see Haider, *Capital and Labor under Fascism*; Rosenstock-Franck, *L'Économie corporative fasciste*; Salvemini, *Under the Axe of Fascism*. Unfortunately few scholars have penetrated beneath the surface of legislative formalities. Representative of the genuflecting official point of view is Pitigliani, *The Italian Corporative State*.

[3] Quoted by Salvemini, *op. cit.*, p. 21. The Charter of Labor (Paragraph

insight is necessary to suspect that this system, despite superficially impressive official vestments, is actually a means for delivering the working class into the control of a machine operating in the interests of the dominant employing group. Only demonstration is needed.

The Fascists had attempted, from the first, to organize occupational associations. In 1920-22, while the Socialist and Catholic unions were declining, the Fascist labor and employer organizations became increasingly stronger. These early "corporations" were mixed associations of employers and workers. After the inauguration of the new syndicate system in 1926, the original Fascist Corporation of Agriculture, with its subsidiary federations of landowners, agricultural technicians, and farm workers, was reorganized into two federations, one representing the landowners, and one the technicians and workers.[4]

The agricultural-workers' organization was at first affiliated with a general national federation of workers of all trades. With the abolition of the latter at the end of 1928 the agricultural laborers were grouped under a special confederation, no longer associated with non-agricultural workers. This organization (the *Confederazione Fascista dei Lavoratori dell'Agricoltura*) is composed of four national "category federations": (1) share-tenants; (2) ordinary wage earners and day

3), to be sure, announces that "syndical or occupational organization is free." It may be that, as Silone says, "the laws exist only for the benefit of law students and foreigners."

[4] For a time there was a hot dispute as to whether cash-tenants and share-tenants should belong to one or the other of the two new organizations. It was finally decided to associate share-tenants with the workers and cash-tenants with the employers. For an official account of the agricultural syndicate organizations see F. Angelini and M. Muzzarini, "L'organizzazione sindacale dei ceti rurali," in Ministero dell'Agricoltura e delle Foreste, *I progressi dell'agricoltura italiana in regime fascista.*

laborers; (3) workers in special agricultural branches (animal husbandry, forestry, etc.); (4) administrative and technical workers in agricultural and forest enterprises.[5] Provincial and local unions of workers in the four categories make up the subordinate structure. The worker-members take no active part in the functioning of the unions; officials are named by and responsible to the government,[6] and are overwhelmingly drawn from the middle class. At the end of 1936 the confederation claimed 2,392,748 members.[7]

Unions of agricultural employers became increasingly active in North Italy after the World War in the fight against the militant workers (and in this mission were allied with the punitive *fasci di combattimento*). They were merged, early in 1922, with the first Fascist general agricultural organization, the Confederation of Agriculture, which, in turn, was affiliated with the National Confederation of Syndical Corporations. In 1926, after the promulgation of the syndical laws, the agricultural employers reorganized, forming an autonomous confederation (*Confederazione Nazionale Fascista degli Agricoltori*). This also comprises four "category federations": (1) employing landowners and cash-tenants; (2) non-cultivating landowners who have let their land; (3) non-employing, cultivating landowners and cash-tenants; (4) managers of agricultural enterprises. Provincial and local organization is similar to that of the workers. Total membership of the confederation at the end of 1936 was 873,500.[8] Close relations are

[5] True at the time of writing. The number and nature of these subordinate federations has changed several times in recent years.

[6] According to *Agricoltura Fascista*, March 4, 1934, the local functionaries of the unions must be "selected with scrupulous care and by agreement with the hierarchy of the Party."

[7] That is, approximately 80 per cent of the total number of tenants and workers represented. Ministry of Corporations, *News Notes*, April 1937, p. 2.

[8] That is, about 20 per cent of the total number of "landowners" and

maintained between the confederation and various agricultural trade associations, such as the federations of agricultural distributive coöperatives, of beet growers, of coöperative wineries and dairies, and the like.

Agricultural experts (economists, agronomists, etc.) were originally united with the confederation of workers. However, in accordance with the wishes of the employers, the experts have been grouped into a separate syndicate attached to the general confederation of "professional men and artists."

Formally, the chief function of this syndicate system is the making of collective labor contracts. Other functions include: representation of employers and workers before the courts; selection of candidates for the Chamber of Deputies; the study of agricultural problems; administration and supervision of social-welfare schemes; collaboration in the government's agricultural program. Each confederation maintains an extensive administrative, economic, and publicity staff. Dues are collected from all employers and workers represented.

Such in bare outline is the complex structure of the syndical organizations in terms of whose functioning the working conditions of agricultural labor presumably are fixed. Commentators write rhapsodically about the syndicates, their achievement of "class collaboration," their mission in giving the rural masses a voice in the life of the nation, their promotion of better living conditions and more efficient production. The hundreds of collective contracts, national and provincial, developed by the confederations, and the thousands of labor disputes settled by their mediation are cited as evidence.[9] But

---

cash-tenants. For a full description of the structure and activities of this confederation, see Confederazione Nazionale Fascista degli Agricoltori, *Dieci anni di attività sindacale 1922-1932*.

[9] By the end of 1936, 73 agricultural labor contracts of a national or

what matters—yet rarely gets the notice of these writers—is the hours of work, the level of wages, the security of the job established under the syndical system. This, not formal structure, demands the attention of the serious inquirer.

HOURS OF WORK

By 1920 many collective labor contracts in industry and agriculture provided for a maximum working day of eight hours. Efforts of labor organizations to legalize the general eight-hour day met with nominal recognition in the decree of March 15, 1923, which stipulated that the normal working hours in all industries were not to exceed eight a day or forty-eight a week. (In agriculture, this maximum was to apply only to hired laborers, not to share-tenants.) However, a decree of June 30, 1926, authorized employers to increase the working day to nine hours, the ninth hour to be paid for at a rate 10 per cent above that for normal hours.[10]

These general regulations are shot through with many qualifications. For instance, the decree of 1923 provides that, in case of technical, seasonal or weather contingencies, a maximum of ten additional hours per week may be required without further compensation. Overtime not in excess of two hours per day or twelve per week may be added to the normal time; this is to be paid for at a rate of 10 per cent higher than that for ordinary hours. Working hours do not include breaks for meals or rest; many agreements stipulate that time spent in going to and coming from the fields (often quite long) also is not included. Furthermore, the legal limits may be exceeded

interprovincial, and 2,226 of a provincial character had been published. Ministry of Corporations, *News Notes,* April 1937, p. 4.

[10] Three peasants of the province of Lecce who in August 1926 distributed printed protests against the nine-hour day were sentenced to prison

when a suspension of work might entail damage to human beings or to production.[11]

Obviously, these qualifications offer employers easy opportunities for prolonging the working day beyond the statutory limit. The significance of the legal maximum thus is practically destroyed. Moreover, the collective contracts generally provide for various daily maxima in different seasons of the year, merely obtaining an *annual average* of eight hours a day. Thus, during the winter months—when in any case it is not possible to carry on much work—the maximum hours are frequently fixed at six a day; during the spring and autumn they are eight, and in the summer, when work is at its heaviest, nine and often ten hours are the rule. This means that the laborers who find employment only in the summer (and these are numerous) are obliged to work well beyond the legal limit without extra compensation. Furthermore, it appears that even these wide legal limits are frequently surpassed by employers who violate the contracts.[12]

WAGES

There are no legal minimum wages in Fascist Italy. The Charter of Labor (Paragraph 12) declares that "wages shall correspond to the normal exigencies of life, to the possibilities of production, and to the output of labor. Wages shall be fixed

---

terms ranging from four to six years. *Corriere della Sera*, July 28, 29, 1927.

[11] International Institute of Agriculture, *Annuaire international de législation agricole, 1923;* International Labour Office, *Collective Agreements in Agriculture*, pp. 87-88.

[12] Paid vacations for agricultural workers in continuous employment for more than one year were introduced in principle in the Charter of Labor. Those actually provided in the collective contracts are short—three to six days, for the most part. Confederazione Fascista dei Lavoratori dell'Agricoltura, *Problemi corporativi del lavoro agricolo nel campo internazionale*, pp. 37 ff.

without reference to any general rules as a matter of agreement between the parties to the collective contracts." The Fascist attitude is that "the Charter of Labor . . . has outmoded all the old theories [of wages]. In the corporative economy there is no minimum wage, as there is no maximum wage. The guarantee of adequate wages lies in the action of the syndicates, the conciliatory action of the corporate organs, the decisions of the labor courts."[13] Mussolini, in a speech on May 26, 1934, gave as the rule for Fascist wage policy: "The greatest possible quantity of labor to the greatest number of workers—ceasing to put the accent on the size of the wage."[14]

Money wages in agriculture and industry have had much the same trend since the World War: decline in 1921-23, then a rise during the period of inflation to 1926. With measures leading to the stabilization of the lira in December 1927, began a period of continual and drastic wage cuts that continued into 1935. During this period the government intervened actively to force down the level of wages. "Spontaneous" cuts were effected in the spring of 1927, and in October 1927 the Fascist party ruled that wages must be reduced by 10 to 20 per cent. Thereafter, additional reductions were made, despite declarations by Mussolini in 1928 and 1931 that none would be permitted. In November 1930 the wages of all government employees were cut by 12 per cent, and the syndical organizations followed this lead by reductions ranging from 8 to 10 per cent in industry and 15 to 20 per cent in agriculture. Further cuts of varying size were imposed afterwards.

In 1935 the general downward movement of wages was

[13] Confederazione Nazionale dei Sindacati Fascisti dell'Agricoltura, *I salari*, pp. 37 ff.

[14] "Nevertheless," according to Haider, *Capital and Labor Under Fascism*, p. 157, "minimum wages are persistently demanded by the working population."

suspended, and the rising cost of living led to moderate advances in 1936 and 1937. Under the terms of a national collective contract between the confederations of agricultural workers and employers, concluded in September 1936, wages of some two million rural wage workers were raised 6 to 9 per cent. A second national contract, announced in May 1937, increased wages by 10 to 12 per cent. These advances, occurring in the face of a marked rise in the prices of consumers' goods and of increased industrial profits, were followed in the press by chants of praise for the generosity of the Duce.[15]

Although the decline in wages was general, agricultural laborers were more seriously affected than workers in industry and commerce. For example, the official indexes of wages of industrial workers and of ordinary male farm laborers show declines of 22 and 28 per cent, respectively, during the period 1928-35.[16]

All commentators agree that there has been a substantial decline in agricultural wages during the last ten years; there is little agreement, however, as to the extent of the decline, or its significance in terms of real income. Mussolini pointed out as early as May 7, 1928: "It is necessary that the Italians should know, that the whole world should know, that the Italian workers and peasants have accepted wage reductions which may be estimated gloriously at some milliards of lire . . ."[17] At a congress of the Confederation of Agricultural Workers in 1932 it was declared that from 1926 to 1932 wages had fallen 30 per cent in Emilia, 34 per cent in Lombardy, and as much as 40 to 50 per cent in certain provinces. A writer in *Lavoro Fascista* (October 26, 1934) points out that con-

[15] *Lavoro Fascista*, September 1936; May 1937.

[16] Istituto Centrale di Statistica, *Bolletino dei Prezzi*, various numbers, 1928-35.

[17] Longobardi, *Land Reclamation in Italy*, p. 181.

tractual wages in various provinces of Sicily fell 10 to 30 per cent from 1930 to 1934. According to the *Lavoro Agricolo Fascista* (the journal of the Agricultural-Workers' Confederation), "There are provinces, such as Milan, Pavia, Cremona, where the reductions have reached as high as 45-60 per cent" (November 29, 1931); "From 1927 to today wages have fallen on the average 45 per cent" (May 15, 1932); "The peasants . . . have seen their wages cut by 50 per cent" (August 7, 1932).

But Fascist writers generally skim lightly over the subject of wage declines. Officially sanctioned wage statistics are often mutually inconsistent, and competent observers are of the opinion that they have a decided upward bias. At any rate, it can be safely assumed that they do not represent conditions to be worse than they actually are. Of course, it is difficult to generalize about wage levels when local conditions and terms of employment vary as much as they do in Italy.

The official statistics (presented in Table 5, p. 114) indicate an average national decline of 38 per cent in nominal wage rates of agricultural day labor in the period 1927-35. In the individual provinces and agricultural occupations the reductions vary considerably (roughly from 20 to 60 per cent), but in every instance they have been serious. For instance, the daily wages of rice weeders (average of eight Northern provinces) fell from 22.50 lire in 1926 to 9.50 lire in 1935; hourly wages of men day laborers in Lombardy dropped from 1.80 lire in June 1927 to 1.27 lire in June 1935; in Calabria, during the same period, from 1.80 lire to 0.92 lire.[18]

[18] For further details in respect of wage rates see International Labour Office, "Statistics of Wages of Agricultural Workers in Various Countries, 1927-1934"; Albertario, *I salari agricoli della Bassa Lombardia 1881-1930;* Arcari, *I salari agricoli in Italia dal 1905 al 1933;* Istituto Centrale di Statistica, *Bolletino dei Prezzi,* various numbers.

TABLE 5.

GENERAL TREND OF AGRICULTURAL WAGES[19]

Wages of ordinary day laborers, male; Annual averages, 1905-35

YEARS	HOURLY WAGES (ISTITUTO CENTRALE DI STATISTICA)[a]		DAILY WAGES (CONFEDERATION OF AGRICULTURAL WORKERS)[b]	
	Amount in lire	*Purchasing power (1913-14 = 100)*	*Amount in lire*	*Purchasing power (1913-14 = 100)*
1905–9	0.18	95		
1910–14	0.22	98		
1913–14	0.23	100	2.43	100
1915–19	0.56	139		
1919	0.88	168	10.62	133.5
1920	1.26	158	11.78	109.7
1921	1.31	153	13.41	102.0
1922	1.47	158	13.08	107.6
1923	1.48	161	12.88	107.3
1924	1.49	157	12.86	100.4
1925	1.61	149	14.13	95.2
1926	1.67	144	14.24	89.6
1927	1.63	155	14.01	98.1
1928	1.52	157	13.05	101.4
1929	1.51	152	12.94	97.7
1930	1.45	149	12.47	96.8
1931	1.26	148	10.49[d]	87.8[d]
1932	1.15	141		
1933	1.08	143		
1934	1.05	146		
1935	1.04[c]	143[c]		

[a] The Istituto in 1934 published series (based on a study by Paola Arcari) of nominal and of real wages of agricultural day laborers for the period 1905-33. But the series of nominal wage rates published more recently by the Istituto does not agree with the Arcari data. In order, therefore, to obtain one index for the entire period 1905-35 it has been necessary to "splice" the two series. The lire data are annual arithmetic means of maximum and minimum wages, as reported periodically by the directors

[19] Sources: Istituto Centrale di Statistica, *Bolletino Mensile di Statistica Agraria e Forestale*, May 1934, *Bolletino dei Prezzi*, various numbers, 1934-35; Confederazione Nazionale dei Sindacati Fascista dell'Agricoltura, *I salari*, pp. 270 ff.

of the *Cattedre Ambulenti di Agricoltura* in each province. The index of purchasing power is based on the official index of the cost of living for 47 cities.

[b] Annual weighted averages of wage rates fixed in collective contracts. The number of workers in each province has served as a basis of weighting. Because of the decline in working hours per day during the period considered, daily rates are selected as more accurate than hourly rates. The cost factor in the purchasing power index is the cost of living index of Milan province. No national cost of living index with a pre-War base, and no index of the rural cost of living, is available.

[c] Average of first nine months.

[d] Average of first six months.

Actual earnings of agricultural labor, in money and produce, have declined even more, however, for the years since 1926 have seen enormous growth both in casual employment and unemployment. Unfortunately, only scattered evidence regarding annual incomes of agricultural workers is available. Thus, for instance, in the southern district of Milan province, the salary of a man in fixed employment was estimated at: 4,800 lire a year in the period 1920-21; 5,070 lire in 1925-26; and 2,940 lire in 1931-32.[20] Employment during only 150-180 days per year is very frequent in the Po basin. A typical agricultural laborer in the province of Forlì was employed only ninety-five days throughout the year 1934 and earned a total of 1,297 lire. It has been stated, further, that many workers in that province, especially in the hills, could earn 1,000 lire a year only with difficulty. Agricultural workers in Sicily in 1934 were said to be unable to find employment for more than 160 days per year, during which period they earned 8 to 9 lire per day.[21]

[20] Giustizia e Libertà, "I braccianti agricoli," pp. 112-18.

[21] *Lavoro Fascista*, October 23, 26, 1934. For further data on annual earnings of peasants and agricultural workers, see *Lavoro Agricolo Fascista*, June 22, 1930; *Lavoro Fascista*, November 1, 1931; Pagani, *I braccianti della valle padana;* Brizi, *Compartecipazione agrarie e contadini partecipanti in Campania e in Lucania.* See also the series of studies of peasant

Texts of the collective agreements often enable employers to alter the nominal tariff wage. For instance, it is possible to shift workers from one category to another in order to alter their wages. Thus, Article 16 of a contract for salaried agricultural workers in the province of Milan (August 1932) states that "the worker who is not capable of the task to which he is assigned may be changed to another category. In case of such shift his wage becomes that of the new category, and from the day of such shift."[22] To be realistic, too, any description of labor conditions based on provisions of the collective agreements must take into account the numerous breaches of such provisions. That violations are not infrequent is shown by the many complaints of workers, guarded though they usually are. The growth of unemployment, particularly, has been attended by increasing violations on the part of employers. This is admitted by the Fascist press. For example, workers "are obliged by the scarcity of jobs to compete with one another to the extent of making contract terms almost meaningless," (*Lavoro Fascista*, May 21, 1929); "Violations continue all along the line," (*Lavoro Agricolo Fascista*, July 31, 1932); "The majority of employers do not respect the tariff wages of the laborers," (*Lavoro Agricolo Fascista*, August 7, 1932); "It is not always easy to make a labor contract, but once completed the difficulty then is to make it observed," (*Lavoro d'Italia*, September 13, 1929). According to *Lavoro Fascista*, May 5, 1929, violations often reduce wages 20 per cent, sometimes 50 per cent, below the contract terms.

During the deflationary period after 1927 the government

---

family living standards published by the Istituto Nazionale di Economia Agraria, *Monografie di famiglie rurali*.

[22] Giustizia e Libertà, "I braccianti agricoli," p. 116.

made vigorous efforts to bring down prices of consumption goods. However, these efforts were decidedly less effective than those to reduce wages.[23] According to the index of the Istituto Centrale di Statistica, real hourly wages in agriculture in 1935 were 9-10 per cent below those of 1928 and 15 per cent below those of 1919. The index of the Agricultural-Workers' Confederation shows 1931 wages to be 13 per cent below those of 1928, 34 per cent below those of 1919, and 12.2 per cent below those of 1913-14. Assuming that the official cost-of-living index is reliable, the wage advances of 1936 and 1937 appear to have done no more than compensate for the increases in living costs since 1934. It is to be noted that these advances came only *after* prices of consumption goods had been rising for nearly two years.

Examination of rates in particular occupations and districts indicates that in some cases real wages fell by as much as one-third between 1927 and 1935. It must be emphasized that these observations relate only to nominal hourly or daily rates. Taking into account also the greatly increased unemployment, frequent violation of contract rates by employers, and the trend toward payment in kind,[24] it is certain that the agricul-

[23] The official cost-of-living index for 50 cities stood at 100 on June 1, 1928, at 74 on August 1, 1934, (the low point since 1927), at 78 on July 1, 1935, at 84 on July 1, 1936, and at 87 on March 1, 1937. The retail-food price index fell from an average of 100 in 1928 to 68 in 1934, then steadily rose to 80 at the end of 1936. Istituto Centrale di Statistica, *Annuario Statistico, 1937*, p. 159. These indexes are not particularly applicable to agricultural workers, but may be taken as an approximation of the general trend of living costs in town and country. Declines of consumption-goods prices in country districts are said to lag several months behind those in cities. Confederazione Nazionale dei Sindacati Fascisti dell'Agricoltura, *I salari*, p. 24. This must be borne in mind in examining the index of real wages of agricultural labor.

[24] For the development of wages in kind, see below, pp. 129-31.

tural laboring population of Italy has suffered a very serious decline in its real income under the Fascist regime.[25]

UNEMPLOYMENT AND UNEMPLOYMENT RELIEF

Agricultural laborers have suffered not only from falling wages but also from reduced chances of finding work. Rural

TABLE 6

UNEMPLOYMENT IN AGRICULTURE AND IN ALL INDUSTRIES[26]

Number of unemployed workers (in thousands) in months of maximum and minimum unemployment, 1922-35

YEARS AND MONTHS	AGRI-CULTURE	ALL IN-DUSTRIES	YEARS AND MONTHS	AGRI-CULTURE	ALL IN-DUSTRIES
1922 Jan.	194		1929 Feb.	194	489
July	49		June	29	193
1923 Jan.	99	392	1930 June	32	322
Aug.	25	179	Dec.	178	642
1924 Jan.	83	281	1931 June	58	574
Sept.	17	116	Dec.	236	982
1925 Feb.	36	157	1932 Feb.	313	1148
Aug.	9	72	June	119	905
1926 July	9	80	1933 Jan.	304	1225
Dec.	50	181	July	110	824
1927 June	24	215	1934 Jan.	333	1158
Dec.	131	414	June	88	831
1928 Jan.	126	439	1935 Jan.	253	1012
July	36	234	June	66	638

[25] Study of the international comparison of real wages and the industrial and agricultural wages in various countries published by the International Labour Office gives good reason to believe that real wages of agricultural workers in Italy are lower than in any other country of Central or Western Europe.

[26] Data for 1922-27, Istituto Centrale di Statistica, *Annuario Statistico, 1928*, p. 263; 1928-34, *Annuario Statistico, 1928-35;* 1935, *Bolletino Mensile di Statistica*, various numbers, 1935. These statistics of unemployment, based on estimates made monthly by officials of labor exchanges, seem subject to a considerable margin of error. Serious errors can creep into the

unemployment was very large in 1921-22, then declined to relatively low levels in 1925-26, and from 1927 to 1934 mounted rapidly. Only after the beginning of 1935 did it fall —a consequence, in large part, of mobilization for the war in Abyssinia. The number of jobless agricultural workers—particularly prominent in the Po basin—has been a large proportion of the total national unemployment. Part-time unemployment has also been large.

Italy was the first country in the world to develop a system of obligatory unemployment insurance providing benefits for all categories of wage earners in industry and agriculture. This was established under a law of October 19, 1919. However, because of alleged difficulties in administering the scheme in the field of agriculture, rural workers have been deprived of unemployment insurance since the end of 1923.

The mounting agricultural unemployment of recent years has obliged the government to provide a variety of aids to the jobless. This has consisted largely of the extension of employment exchanges, encouragement of seasonal migration to regions where workers can be temporarily absorbed, recourse to the "tax in workers," and, most important, large-scale development of public works. (In one sense, the military measures in 1935-36 must be considered as a type of "public works" for the relief of unemployment.) At the same time

estimates in consequence of the method of collecting the data; furthermore, observers have pointed to contradictions between the regional estimates and the final figures published by the central statistical organization. See Salvemini, "Italian Unemployment Statistics," and *Under the Axe of Fascism*, pp. 238 ff., 260 ff., 282-83; Pagani, *I braccianti della valle padana*, pp. 61-62. It should be noted, too, that these data do not take account of the reduction of wage work among small peasant proprietors.

At any rate, taken at their face value the data indicate that 10-15 per cent of all agricultural laborers have been out of work during the winters 1931-35. This is relatively higher than unemployment among industrial workers.

efforts have been made to transform the agricultural wage-workers into share-croppers or tenants, by settling workers and their families on reclaimed lands and by endeavoring to extend the share-cropping system.[27] Emigration, formerly so important as an outlet for the poverty-stricken agricultural workers and peasants, has been made increasingly difficult since the World War. Countries to which Italians formerly went in large numbers have raised immigration barriers. But the Fascist regime itself has taken drastic steps to reduce emigration.

The early system of government employment exchanges, instituted in 1919, was suspended at the end of 1923. For several years the national confederation of workers' syndicates administered such exchanges, but the increasing unemployment made imperative the restoration of a State system. In December 1927, communal employment offices, directed by commissions of employers and employees under the control of the local Fascist organization, were inaugurated. These agencies have the exclusive privilege of placing workers.[28] All unemployed workers are required to register; workers accepting employment offered through any other intermediary are sub-

[27] That is, as Fascist leaders say, to "deproletarianize" the wageworkers. (See below, pp. 128 ff.) An attempt to reduce the number of women workers, and some tendency toward prohibiting the introduction of labor-saving machinery, are also observable. The London *Times* of June 19, 1935, reported: "Milan, June 18. In order to diminish as far as possible unemployment among Italian laborers the Inter-Syndical Committee has decided that no 'mechanical' means of any kind whatever are to be used for the next harvest. All the work is to be done by hand."

[28] Special national and interprovincial agencies for the placement of workers in the wheat, rice, and olive harvests have also been set up. In practice, it seems that the employment system is decidedly less effective in the South than in the North. For further information on the exchanges, see Oblath, "The Campaign Against Unemployment in Italy," pp. 707-13; Campese, *Il Fascismo contro la disoccupazione*, pp. 79-145.

ject to heavy fines. (Still it appears that many workers do not register for fear of being deported to their home communities.) Unemployed members of the Fascist party are given preference in placement.[29]

Since 1928 municipal officials have been authorized to expel from the towns and send back to their native communities all unemployed workers who have no immediate prospect of employment. There is obviously less concern about the presence of unemployed in the country than in the cities.

The government has attempted to control internal seasonal migration of workers by establishing a special Commissariat for Internal Migration and Colonization. Employment contracts are fixed under the supervision of this authority, and workers are prevented from going to districts where no employment is to be had. Firms responsible for executing state-subsidized works must request the labor exchanges to supply the workers needed, and the Commissariat may require that a certain quota of such laborers be immigrants from other provinces.[30]

The Fascist authorities have also resorted to the "tax in workers" (*imponibile di mano d'opera*) as a method of combating unemployment in certain of the Northern provinces.

[29] A law of March 5, 1935, introduced the *libretto di lavoro*, an employment book containing information on the worker's past record, war service, Fascist affiliations, education, etc. Each employed person must have such a book, and those not in possession thereof may not be registered by the employment exchanges.

[30] The seasonal migration of agricultural workers from one province to another is large, although not so great as before the World War. It amounted to 559,000 persons in 1910, and averaged about 260,000 annually in 1929-34. Laborers migrating for the wheat harvests in the North and in Sicily, and for the weeding and harvesting of rice in the North comprise the bulk of this movement. See Affricano, "Lo sviluppo delle migrazioni interne e la politica di ruralizzazione"; Commissariato per le Migrazioni e la Colonizzazione Interna, *Le migrazioni interne, 1934*.

This "tax"—which consists in obliging agricultural employers, under the terms of collective contracts, to employ a minimum number of workers per unit area of their cultivated land—had been developed in the North on a large scale by the radical workers' unions in the years of widespread unemployment before and immediately after the World War. The "tax" principally served the purpose of rationing jobs among a large number of workers who otherwise would have been unemployed. Agriculturalists found this an irksome burden, and for a time after the institution of the Fascist regime it appeared that it might be dropped altogether. But the urgencies of unemployment have forced the Fascists to maintain it, though without enthusiasm and less effectively than in the past. The burden of the "tax" is not so heavy as it was in the years immediately following the War; employers may accept the obligatory employment in those months when they are particularly in need of labor, rather than in the slack season; furthermore, they are permitted to select the individuals to be employed, thus diminishing the rationing value of the system for the unemployed workers in general.[31]

During the period of depression an extensive public-works program—road building, land reclamation, reforestation, construction of buildings, aqueducts and the like—has been undertaken. State expenditures for this purpose have averaged about

[31] For instance, the average minimum number of workers to be employed per 100 hectares of farm land in eight localities of the Po region in 1920-21 was 32.8; in 1931-32 it was 27.7. Albertario, "L'imponibile di mano d'opera nell'economia agraria del bassopiano lombardo." See also Haider, *Capital and Labor Under Fascism*, pp. 210-11; Giustizia e Libertà "I braccianti agricoli," pp. 116-17. According to a writer in *Lavoro Facista*, August 30, 1936, "The necessity of extending the 'tax in workers' has been much discussed . . . by the Grand Council, the syndical organizations, and students of labor. . . . There has been much talk . . . but up to now nothing has been done."

2,000,000,000 lire per year since 1930, declining in 1934-35 and being drastically reduced in 1936. The total number of days of work thus provided is, in millions: *1931*, 39; *1932*, 42; *1933*, 51; *1934*, 45; *1935*, 39; *1936*, 32.[32] This has meant an absorption of not more than 20 per cent of all unemployed workers.

In recent years the Commissariat for Internal Migration and Colonization has also endeavored to settle permanently agricultural workers and their families on reclaimed lands and in the colonies. So far, however, this has been of slight significance. The total number of families settled in internal zones (largely in the Agro Pontino, Venetia, Emilia, Lombardy, and Sardinia) during the years October 1930 to October 1936 was only 8,857, comprising 70,367 persons.[33] The settlement of families in the African colonies has been quite insignificant.[34] Migration of Italians to foreign countries, permanent or temporary—formerly the most important means of reducing the pressure of population on the country's slender resources—has fallen off very markedly since the War, not only because of restrictions imposed abroad, but also because of the hostile attitude of the Fascist government to permanent emigration.[35]

[32] Istituto Centrale di Statistica, *Annuario Statistico*, *1935*, p. 237; *1936*, p. 199. Outlays for military purposes since 1930 have been more than double those for public works.

[33] See above, p. 101.

[34] Commissariato per le Migrazioni, *Le migrazioni interne*, *1934*, p. cii. For these purposes of internal and external colonization, the Commissariat pays settlement bonuses and helps to defray costs of travel and of land improvement.

[35] In the period 1901-13 the average annual number of emigrants from Italy was 627,000. Since 1922 it has declined as follows (annual averages): *1922-24*, 345,000; *1925-27*, 257,000; *1928-30*, 193,000; *1931-33*, 111,000; *1934-36*, 56,000. Istituto Centrale di Statistica, *Annuario Statistico*, *1937*, p. 38. The rural population supplied a smaller proportion of the emigrants since the War than before. Most of the recent emigration has

Emigrant remittances have declined correspondingly.[36]

Distress among unemployed workers is relieved to a slight extent through the distribution of relief funds in particularly depressed districts by the syndical organizations.

SOCIAL INSURANCE AND SOCIAL WELFARE INSTITUTIONS

Agricultural workers, although not insured against unemployment, have been entitled since 1917 to benefits in case of accident, since 1919 to old-age and invalidity pensions, and since 1927 to insurance against tuberculosis.[37] These schemes are supported by compulsory contributions from employers as well as workers. Benefits in all cases are quite small.[38] In addition to the government-supported insurance systems, the syndi-

---

been to continental European countries—consisting particularly of temporary migration to France. Since 1931, however, this movement has been much reduced. For discussions of Fascist emigration policy see Oblath, "Italian Emigration and Colonisation Policy"; Campese, *Il Fascismo contro la disoccupazione*, pp. 249 ff.; Salvemini, "Can Italy Live at Home?"

[36] Remittances to Italy are estimated to have fallen 75 per cent from 1919 to 1932. See Nicolai, *Les Remises des emigrants italiens*, pp. 150 ff.

[37] According to recent press reports a system of contributory maternity insurance, which has been available to industrial women workers, will shortly be extended to agriculture. Some 600,000 rural women are expected to participate in the scheme. *Giornale d'Italia*, July 28, 1936.

[38] All workers and share-tenants are insured against occupational accidents. In case of accidental death, the survivors receive 6,000-8,000 lire; in case of 90 per cent disability, an indemnity of 5,000-6,000 lire is paid; temporary disability is indemnified by a daily allowance of 3-4 lire. Wage workers and *compartecipanti* are entitled to old-age and invalidity pensions; share-tenants have been excluded since 1923. The pensions are based on the amount of contributions by the insured and his employer. In 1928-32 the average old-age pension was 700-1,000 lire per year; the average invalidity pension was 600-1,000 lire. Granting of the pensions is made the occasion of patriotic celebrations by the Fascists. Contributions for accident insurance are paid entirely by employers; those for old-age, invalidity, and tuberculosis insurance are divided equally between employers and workers. Information from the national institutions for social insurance, and from International Labour Office, *Industrial and Labour Information*, June 18, 1934, p. 412.

cal organizations now provide for further aid through the establishment of sickness funds.[39] But some observers have grave doubts about the actual effectiveness of the insurance system, at any rate in the South. They declare that its operation in the agricultural field has left much to be desired: too frequently payments of contributions have been evaded; it is difficult to keep account of the insured workers; many workers and peasants are imperfectly informed about the nature of the benefits.[40] Furthermore, the funds of the insurance institutions have been tapped increasingly by the government as a convenient and not unimportant source of credit. Only a fraction of the receipts in recent years have been paid out as benefits to the insured.

The Fascist government has fostered the development of a number of institutions concerned with "social welfare," education, recreation, and propaganda. From the standpoint of the rural population the most important of these are the *Balilla* and *Dopolavoro* organizations, the National Institute for Maternity and Infancy, the *Patronato Nazionale*, and the National Society of War Veterans. The *Opera Nazionale Balilla* provides for the physical, military, and patriotic education of children and young persons. It has a pronounced military, nationalistic character, and aims to instill in the youth a devotion and obedience to the Fascist system. The *Dopolavoro* concerns itself with education, sport, and recreation for workers. The maternity and infancy organization is intended to assist mothers during and after child-birth, and to protect infants of poor mothers. The *Patronato Nazionale* (founded in 1910)

[39] Since October 1935, labor-union sickness funds have been set up in 58 provinces. It is said that 1,800,000 agricultural workers and share-tenants and their families are entitled to benefits from these funds.

[40] See Roberti, "Lo sviluppo delle assicurazioni sociali in agricoltura."

gives free assistance to workers involved in social insurance controversies, and also assists insured persons in claiming their rights to benefits. Finally, the *Opera Nazionale dei Combattenti*, originally organized at the end of the War, provides for the economic welfare of World War veterans. This society has acquired particular prominence by reason of its supervision of land-reclamation projects and its acquisition of land for settlement by ex-service men and their families.[41]

These institutions doubtless make contributions toward the general welfare, but they are probably more significant as potent agencies for the dissemination of Fascist propaganda. They appear, however, to be less effective in the country than in the cities. Some writers have emphasized that their services constitute an important addition to the real income of the rural population. Closer examination of rural living standards in recent years and of welfare-organization activities (particularly in the South) suggest that such opinion must be heavily discounted.

LABOR DISPUTES

As noted above, since 1926 all disputes between employers and workers must first be referred to a mechanism of conciliation, and, if not thus settled, then must be submitted to special courts for compulsory arbitration. Resort to any other method for settling labor disputes is illegal.[42] During the eight years 1927-35, 771 disputes relating to terms of collective contracts were submitted to the Ministry of Corporations for conciliation; 86 involved agricultural agreements. Of these 86 disputes, 69 were settled, 11 were not settled, and 6 were dropped or held up. To November 1933, 14 disputes involving collec-

[41] See above, pp. 30, 93, 100.

[42] However, strikes are not entirely unknown; there were 56 in agriculture during 1927-33. Istituto Centrale di Statistica, *Annuario Statistico*, various years.

tive contracts had been settled by the labor courts; 2 of these related to agriculture.[43] The number of labor disputes concerning individuals alone has been very large and has tended to increase.[44] This probably is an indication, but only partially so, of the extent to which contracts were violated. It would seem that, given the present system of labor organization and extensive unemployment, a worker who has suffered what he believes to be a breach of his contractual working conditions would hesitate before making a complaint. Probably only the bolder or more desperate workers would decide to denounce violations of which they have been the victims.

It is interesting to note the tendencies reflected in the decisions of the labor courts. In the few cases involving agricultural collective contracts that have been decided by the courts the procedure was virtually the same: first, the employers' syndical organization demanded a reduction in wages; then the workers' syndical officials offered to accept a reduction, but not so great as that desired by the employers; and finally the courts either fixed the reduction at the level suggested by the workers' officials, or else compromised between their proposal and that of the employers.[45] In view of the identity of the political controls over the courts and the syndical organizations, the court verdicts cannot be other than a formal registra-

[43] *International Labour Review*, October 1934, pp. 509-28; Istituto Centrale di Statistica, *Bollettino Mensile di Statistica*, July 1935, p. 548; *Annuario Statistico, 1937*, p. 168, 170.

[44] The number of individual complaints in all industries has averaged nearly 200,000 for the past several years. In 1936, there were 88,230 complaints concerning agricultural workers. The syndicate organization settled 51,348 of these in favor of the complainants, and 1,527 unfavorably. The labor magistrates settled 3,246 favorably and 206 unfavorably. Over 31,000 complaints were abandoned or remained unsettled. Istituto Centrale di Statistica, *Annuario Statistico, 1937*, p. 168.

[45] For further details, see Salvemini, *Under the Axe of Fascism*, pp. 67 ff., 224-25.

tion of decisions made in higher quarters. However, Fascist commentators pretend to take seriously the activities of the labor courts and point to them as an example of "class collaboration in practice."

"DEPROLETARIZATION": THEORY AND PRACTICE

A cardinal goal in the avowed social-economic policy of the Fascist regime is *sbracciantizzazione*, or "deproletarization," of the agricultural masses. According to the leading agricultural economist of Fascism,

> it is morally, politically, and economically necessary to develop stable relationships between the worker and the land that he cultivates. . . . Thus we can have in the country, not nomadic casual laborers, forever uncertain of the next day, forever agitated in the search of a higher wage rendered illusory by uncertain employment, but *genuine peasants attached to the soil*, loving the soil, *who do not ask the impossible*, *who know how to content themselves*, certain in any case of the necessities of life.[46]

The ideal of the old Socialist movement is declared to have been destruction of small, individual proprietorship and share-tenancy and development of a proletarian army of landless workers. Fascism must seek the opposite goal, "because, as in France, landed property would always be saved by the many little owners."[47]

According to official avowals this is to be achieved by "fixing the workers to the soil": transforming day laborers into workers on long-time contracts and into *compartecipanti*, and ex-

[46] Arrigo Serpieri (former Undersecretary for Land Reclamation) in a speech before the Corporation of Agriculture. See Serpieri, *La legge sulla bonifica integrale nel primo anno di applicazione*, pp. 229-30. (Italics by C. T. S.)

[47] A landowner in a discourse at the Convegno per la Bonifica Integrale, Florence, May 21-22, 1934. R. Accademia dei Georgofili, "Convegno per la bonifica integrale," p. 440.

panding share-tenancy and small peasant proprietorship. Insofar as practical, the collective contracts are to provide for a greater proportion of wage payments in kind and for the extension of share-cropping.

> All the syndical corporative activities of the Fascist workers' organizations, in all sectors . . . are directed toward this objective . . . to transform the proletarian who is not and cannot be nationalist, and even less Fascist, into a type of artisan who can be made to feel the nature of property.[48]

Peasant proprietorship is to be protected and extended by vigorous encouragement of production and by making available to small colonists large areas of reclaimed land.

But practice has hardly been faithful to the theory.

Certainly, progress has been made in "fixing workers to the soil." But it has been almost entirely in the direction of furthering the practice of paying wages in kind and of extending the share-cropping system—additional factors in reducing the mobility and bargaining strength of the wage earners. Only an insignificant number of wageworkers have advanced to the status of tenants, much less to that of small landowners. Indeed, far from finding reinforcement under Fascism, the peasant economy has been declining seriously.[49]

More and more frequently, when wages are cut, the reduction is made largely in the cash portion of the wage. Thus larger shares are paid in produce. The uncertainty of the wage earner's income is thereby increased. With regard to the products that he cannot consume directly he is exposed to all the usual market risks.

In this respect Luigi Razza, formerly president of the Fascist Agricultural-Workers' Confederation, pointed out: "It

[48] Luigi Razza, in *Ibid.*, p. 358.
[49] See below, pp. 132 ff.

is necessary to return to the ancient system [of payment in kind]. . . . The worker must have the pride of carrying home to his wife and children the fruits of his labor—bread, wine, and condiments. And the agricultural employers thus need not run to the banks every week to get money for wage payments."[50] And a writer in *Popolo d'Italia* (April 7, 1929) declared that the payment of wages in money is "anti-economic, reminiscent of Socialist and Populist demagogy." The *Lavoro Agricolo Fascista* (October 6, 1929) reports a peasant as having declared in a meeting in Milan province: "The best system was that of abolishing all payments in kind and paying in cash every two weeks." To this a syndicate official replied: "This proposition is an open contradiction of all the doctrine and practice of Fascism."

The tendency, however, is to go further and to urge the wider adoption of the contract of *compartecipazione*, or share-cropping. As observed before, the cropper cultivates under the direction of the employer, has no independence in selection of the crops or method of work, and is subject to the employer's discipline. The cropper is therefore a dependent worker, paid in kind instead of in cash, with no guarantees as to income or working hours, and more firmly bound to the employer than the wage laborer. Indeed, the approach of serfdom is too close to have escaped the attention even of Fascist writers. Thus a syndicate official has held that "Fascist collaboration" is necessary to escape the risk of putting the workers at the mercy of the employers, of returning to feudal servitude.[51] A speaker before a congress of Milanese workers said: "In not a few cases *compartecipazione* degenerates and comes to represent in the hands of less correct proprietors a

[50] *Lavoro Agricolo Fascista*, September 20, 1931.
[51] Aimi, *Dalla scomparsa del salariato alla corporazione*, p. 11.

means of imposing on the croppers heavy uncompensated burdens. . . . Who wonders, then, that . . . so many peasants and workers want payment in cash, considering it as a delivery from servitude?"[52]

But the Fascist syndical leaders press for an extension of this system. While much is said about the advantages it gives to the workers, such as greater security of income and an approach to independent ownership, it is clear that the interests of employers are not forgotten. It is no accident that this effort has occurred at a time of financial difficulty for landlords and employer farmers.[53] Furthermore, *compartecipazione* is declared to be "a safeguard for the land itself against the risks of sudden convulsion and upheaval."[54] The "safeguarding" of property rights and the grinding-down of real wages—this is the reality of Fascist labor policy.

[52] *Lavoro Agricolo Fascista*, May 21, 1929. For Fascist expositions of *compartecipazione*, see Aimi, *op. cit.*, and *Verso la scomparsa del salariato*; Pagani, *Le compartecipazione agricole del Mantovano*.

[53] Share-cropping is spoken of as providing low-cost labor. "Fortunately this disparity [between rigid wages and falling agricultural prices] was notably diminished by the wide extension of remuneration based on participation by the worker in the product or on payment in kind." Serpieri and Mortara, "Politica agraria fascista," p. 258.

[54] Ministry of Corporations, *News Notes*, September 1932. On March 25, 1930, the Fascist Grand Council, in considering the situation of the agricultural workers of the Po basin, recommended that share-cropping contracts be adopted as far as possible. The confederations of agricultural workers and employers signed an accord on October 25, 1934, which provides, among other things, for the substitution wherever possible of share-cropping for wage contracts; and where this is impractical, for increased payment of wages in kind. Again, on December 23, 1935, the two confederations agreed to develop collective contracts of *compartecipazione* in Sicily. In October 1936, the confederations concluded such a contract. This provides for the transformation of short-term tenancy contracts into share-cropping agreements, the minimum period of which is to be three years. The landlord is to receive 66 per cent of the wheat and 50 per cent of the beans produced. See *News Notes*, September 1932; December 1934; January 1936; *Lavoro Fascista*, October 8, 1936.

VII: Peasants and Proprietors

The Corporation is the bosses. . . . When there's any dirty work to be done, the bosses don't do it individually any more; individualism is a thing of the past; nowadays when there's dirty work, it's like this: Three of the bosses get together; one represents the peasants, another the Super-Class Authority, and a third boss represents the bosses, and the three of them are the Corporation. . . .

—IGNAZIO SILONE[1]

FASCIST doctrine and practice differ in important respects. "Deproletarization" has not led to a strengthening of existing small proprietorship, nor to a wider diffusion of land ownership. Rather, the Fascist era has seen an extension of share-cropping, increasing difficulties for peasant proprietors (especially in the South), and growing subordination of the rural masses to the interests of absentee ownership. The widely heralded "social duties" of landed proprietorship have remained mere rhetoric.

LAND TENURE

To be sure, the Italian census data show a decline of nearly two millions in the number of farm wage workers between 1921 and 1931. Fascist commentators frequently point to this as evidence that the avowed policy of "deproletarization" is being effected. Even allowing for exaggeration due to official and technical bias, it would appear that there has been a decline in the category of wage labor.[2] But the number of "operating

[1] *Mr. Aristotle* (Robert M. McBride and Company, New York, 1935). Reprinted by permission of the publishers.

[2] The occupational data doubtless are subject to error because of the difficulty in classifying persons engaged in several occupations, such as men who

owners" actually fell nearly half a million in the same period. Inasmuch as other data point conclusively to an increase in peasant proprietorship in the period 1915-26,[3] a reasonable inference is that there was a serious reduction during 1926-31—that is, in the years when the regime was supposedly strengthening the small peasants. Moreover, "we have no statistics for the period after 1931, but there is reason to believe that in these last years there has been continuing decline in the number of small cultivating proprietors."[4]

On the other hand, the number of cash- and share-tenants rose by something under 400,000 during 1921-31. It seems likely that many tenants who became landowners during and immediately after the War have been forced by economic difficulties in recent years to return to their old status. There is no evidence whatever to show that an appreciable number of farm laborers have become tenants or landowners.[5]

While the various forms of tenancy have been increasing

---

cultivate a small farm of their own and also work for others, or women who are both housewives and wageworkers. In this respect see the doubts raised by F. Coletti, in *Corriere della Serra*, December 25, 1932, regarding the great decline in wageworkers. Political bias probably affects these data also. One need merely recall that it was in the interests of powerful political groups in 1921 to have evidence of a large mass of wageworkers, whereas the opposite was true in 1931. As late as 1927, one of the official social insurance institutions—in making a survey of the number of persons eligible for tuberculosis insurance—discovered more than 4,500,000 rural wageworkers. See *Zeitschrift für die gesamte Versicherungswissenschaft*, April 1, 1934, p. 114.

[3] See above, pp. 27 ff.

[4] N. Mazzocchi-Alemanni, in R. Accademia dei Georgofili, "Convegno per la bonifica integrale," p. 391. For data on the occupational structure of the rural population in 1921 and 1931, see Istituto Centrale di Statistica, *Censimento della popolazione, 1 dicembre 1921; Censimento generale della popolazione . . . 21 aprile 1931*, Vol. IV, Part 2.

[5] The question then arises: What became of the 2,000,000 persons who had been rural wageworkers in 1921? It is apparent that they did not shift to other agricultural occupations, nor that any appreciable number emigrated permanently. Examination of the occupational structure of the popu-

in prominence, the contractual position of tenants has deteriorated. Terms of share-tenancy agreements concluded since 1922 are decidedly less favorable to the peasants than those developed immediately after the War. A. Marabini[6] cites the more important clauses of two contracts for share-tenancy in the province of Bologna, one (a) effective in 1920, and the other (b) in 1929: *management of the farm*—(a) subject to approval of the two parties, (b) exclusively in the hands of the proprietor; *expenditures for fertilizers and insecticides*—(a) borne by the proprietor, (b) divided equally between tenant and proprietor; *farm animals*—(a) provided by the proprietor, (b) provided by both tenant and proprietor; *cost of maintaining dykes, ditches, and drains*—(a) borne by the proprietor, (b) borne by the tenant; *costs of transportation*—(a) if for products belonging to the proprietor, then borne entirely by him; if for jointly owned products, then divided in the same proportions in which the products are shared; (b) borne entirely by the tenant; *division of the products*—(a) the tenant receives 60 per cent of the wheat, 60-65 per cent of the corn, 65 per cent of the chestnuts, 60-70 per cent of the grapes, 60 per cent of the tobacco, sugar beets, tomatoes, beans; (b) all products are divided equally between the two parties, but premiums for unusually large production of tobacco, sugar beets, tomatoes and beans are to be given to the tenant. The first contract was developed by the Federterra (the Socialist farm-workers' union), and the second by the Fascist syndical authorities.

---

lation in 1921 and 1922 indicates a rise of about 1,000,000 in the number of persons occupied in urban enterprises, and of more than 2,000,000 in the number of persons not gainfully occupied. This suggests that a considerable proportion of the former wage earners drifted into the category of the permanently unemployed.

[6] In "La mezzadria in Italia," pp. 220-21.

Moreover, the extension of the Fascist labor organizations' control over the fixing of tenancy contracts terms is quite different from what the tenants had been led to expect. An act of April 3, 1933, provides that the legal principles applicable to collective labor agreements are to hold also for cash- and share-tenant contracts concluded by the syndicates. But any notion that this might mean that share-tenant contracts must guarantee to tenants a minimum income, maximum working hours, extra pay for extra work and insurance benefits, is immediately dispelled by the qualification that the contracts concluded "must be adjusted to local customs and conditions and may not contain norms relating to wages, hours of work, vacations, or other provisions of collective labor contracts that do not accord with the nature of the landlord-tenant relationship."[7] This act was supplemented (May 13, 1933) by a "Charter of Share Tenancy," embodying basic rules for share-farming agreements. Examination of the "Charter's" terms, too, indicates that the landlords have been victorious, and that the tenants have lost most of the concessions that they had won in the years immediately after the War. For example, it specifies that tenant contracts have a duration of only one year, that they may be abrogated on six months notice, that the administration of the farm is absolutely in the hands of the owner, that the tenant is responsible for all the farm work, even if outside labor must be hired, that all members of the tenant's household are subject to the terms of the contract (and thus that the agreement would be broken if any member were to leave the farm).[8]

[7] Rosenstock-Franck, *L'Économie corporative fasciste*, pp. 100-102, 272-76.

[8] The basic character of the share-tenant contract has long been a subject of debate in Italy. Three viewpoints, held respectively by Socialists, Catholic Populists, and the landlords, may be distinguished: (1) it is a labor contract,

The Fascist policy of enclosing common lands, too, has raised barriers between land and peasants. For centuries the inhabitants of many rural communities had possessed rights of pasturage, cutting wood, watering stock, and even of cultivation and habitation, on certain nominally private lands. These *usi civici*—legacies of feudal land tenure—existed in about half of the communes in Italy (being particularly prominent in the former Papal States and the southern provinces) and were an important source of income for thousands of small peasants. With the development of commercial agriculture, they had become increasingly irksome to the nominal proprietors (whose titles in many cases were based on usurpations by their feudal predecessors), inasmuch as they tended to limit authority and income and complicated transfer of titles. Pre-Fascist governments had sought to settle this problem in favor of the landlords, but these attempts were defeated by peasant resistance. Success was reserved for the Fascist government: under the terms of a decree of May 22, 1924, steps have been taken to abolish the *usi civici* on private lands.[9] By the end of 1936, unencumbered titles to 146,000 hectares had been granted to private individuals, and 44,000 hectares had been transferred

---

and the share-tenant therefore ought to be guaranteed an adequate return for his labor, both in good and bad crop years; (2) it is a contract for hire of the farm property, and therefore payment by the tenant for its use ought to be reduced to fixed amounts of produce; (3) it is a co-partnership contract, and the landlord is the ultimately authoritative partner. The "Charter" definitely represents the last point of view.

[9] It was provided that all communal bodies and individuals claiming such rights must give judicial proof by April 1928 of the continuous existence of their claims since at least the end of the eighteenth century. On establishing such proof, the communal bodies surrendering their rights are to be compensated by receiving a portion of the land in fee simple, and individuals are to be paid small cash amounts by the nominal owners for a limited number of years.

outright to communes.[10] Here again, the great landlords and wealthier farmers have gained at the expense of poor peasants. There is no denying that abolition of the *usi civici* in many cases has had technical advantages (as when the land was overburdened by excessive pasturing). Yet it remains that very many peasants with little or no land have been deprived of pasturage and firewood, and that such small cash compensation as they have received is poor amends for their losses.

In practice, the widely publicized land reclamation and improvement schemes of the Fascists have offered little land to the rural masses. As noted above (Chapter V), they have not even led to any appreciable settlement of landless rural workers as tenants. The unfortunate consequences of land improvement for many poor peasants, particularly in the mountainous areas, must also be taken into account. And the suggestion that the reclamation program would lead to a reduction of the great estates through forced sales or expropriation has not been realized. No significant amount of land has been sold by the big proprietors for the purpose of raising funds to carry out improvement projects, and they have had no need whatever to be worried by the demagogues' talk of the "social duties" of proprietorship. By the end of 1935 only 27,000 hectares—all in the region of the Pontine marshes—had been expropriated because of the landowners' failure to meet "reclamation obligations."[11]

[10] Istituto Centrale di Statistica, *Annuario Statistico, 1937*, p. 62. See Acerbo, *Il riordinamento degli usi civici nel Regno;* N. de Rensis, "Il riordinamento degli usi civici" in Federzoni, *I problemi attuali.*

[11] The landowners were compensated, of course. Information from the Undersecretariat for Land Reclamation. However, the government has been decidedly less hesitant to apply eviction measures to small proprietors who are in arrears in paying taxes or private debts. The number of judicial sales of rural houses and land has been rising steadily in recent years: in *1927*

Occasionally, however, landed proprietors have been inclined to take seriously the rhetoric in respect of "social duties." Thus, a Fascist writer reminds the syndicate leaders that they must not misunderstand the nature of "class collaboration":

There are still some individuals, who, although belonging to the Party and to the Fascist syndicates, have not yet been entirely purged of the democratic or socialist venom, and who think that corporative collaboration means that the proprietors must renounce all or part of the rights belonging to them as owners of the land and managers of the enterprises. . . . The landowners have not only the right, but also the Fascist duty, of remaining in their superior positions as leaders. It is their duty to protect their hierarchical positions against all challengers. . . . And they must be *intransigeant* in matters of discipline, respect, obedience, esteem. . . .[12]

But the syndicate leaders have taken pains to assure landlords that their lot really will not be an unhappy one under Fascism. For example, Lugi Razza (former president of the Agricultural-Workers' Confederation, later Minister of Public Works) found it necessary to point out in 1934:

We are so little against property that one of the fundamental characteristics of our agricultural policy is to make the disinherited also property owners, and the corporative system certainly is not state socialism. . . . This ought above all to reassure those who fear that the Corporate State is a kind of Trojan horse in the citadel of private property, a horse whose inhabitants are the leaders of the workers' syndicates![13]

---

it was 1,652; in *1934*, 10,328; in *1935*, 11,592. Istituto Centrale di Statistica, *Annuario Statistico*, various years, 1928-37.

[12] Pesce, *Contadini d'Italia*, p. 87.

[13] R. Accademia dei Georgofili, "Convegno per la bonifica integrale," p. 385.

It is not surprising, then, that most Italian farm land is still owned by relatively few proprietors. According to the latest agricultural census (that of 1930), 36 per cent of the 4,200,000 farm enterprises in Italy are less than one hectare in size, and 55 per cent are from one to ten hectares. Yet these two classes of farms together comprise only a third of all the agricultural land. That is, two-thirds of the land is controlled by 9 per cent of the farms.[14] It is likely that a census referring to individual proprietors rather than enterprises would reveal even greater concentration of ownership. The farm tax rolls data published for the last time by the Istituto Centrale di Statistica in 1927[15] suggest the following distribution of agricultural land:

	Percentage of Farm Proprietors	*Percentage of Farm Land Held*
Dwarf- and small-holders	87.3	13.2
Petty proprietors	9.3	18.5
Medium proprietors	2.9	26.4
Large proprietors	0.5	41.9
	100.0	100.0

Thus, the peasant masses of Italy remain, as before, separated from control of the land, but with even less hope of rising in the economic scale, at home or abroad. However, the regime has now undertaken to show them the way to a new promised land. The war on Abyssinia from its beginning was depicted as a war for land and labor, for "proletarian Italy." Conquered Abyssinia is to give liberty, land, and bread to the

[14] Istituto Centrale di Statistica, *Censimento generale dell'agricoltura italiana al 19 marzo 1930. Censimento delle aziende agricole.* The concentration of proprietorship is most pronounced in the peninsular South, where but 6 per cent of the farms comprise 63 per cent of the land.

[15] In *Annuario Statistico, 1927*, p. 318.

Italian masses. Very likely, the government will make a show of peasant colonization by subsidizing a limited number of settlers in a highly favorable region—a project that must yield great publicity values. But enormous difficulties of climatic, military, and, above all, economic nature would seem to stand in the way of extensive peasant colonization.[16] Land will be taken from the natives, certainly, but its control and its fruits in all probability will pass into the hands of big concessionaries, colonization and plantation companies, and financial institutions.

RURAL COÖPERATION

In November 1922, Mussolini explained his attitude toward the coöperative movement as follows: "Coöperation must not be considered as an organization contrary to the principles of freedom, understood in the sense of the free play of commercial and industrial activity, but as a practical means of combating all forms of monopoly harmful to the consumer by the sincere application of the fundamental principle of free competition."[17] For nearly two years before this statement was made, Mussolini's followers had been carrying on open warfare against the workers' coöperative movement. As an observer explained, the activities of the coöperative movement "are of course menacing many vested interests, and it is no wonder that coöperation has numerous enemies; the profiteers have launched an army of hooligans against the coöperatives, and many of their buildings have been burned down; the kept

[16] Colonization of the high plain of Asmara (Eritrea) is suggestive in this respect. It is similar physically to the Abyssinian areas available to European farmers and has been open to settlers for decades. Yet only an insignificant number of Italian small farmers are established there.

[17] Quoted by Lloyd, *The Co-operative Movement in Italy*, pp. 108-9.

press accuses them of exploiting the Government and of anti-patriotism."[18]

After the "March on Rome" the Fascist regime completed the destruction of the Socialist coöperative league, suppressed all other societies with anti-Fascist leanings, and erected its own system of coöperatives. In 1925, Lloyd[19] wrote:

> All over Italy there is to be found evidence of the savage attacks on co-operative societies. The writer spoke with leaders who had been driven from their homes and their life work. He heard of many who had been cruelly beaten and of some who had been killed. He saw premises which had been burnt down and others which had been despoiled. In many cases societies had, either voluntarily or under compulsion, changed their allegiance, had disowned their officials and leaders, and accepted in their stead nominees of the Fascist party.

Of the 8,000 societies affiliated with the [Socialist] *Lega* in 1922, only 2,000 remained in August 1923, "and those, for the most part, were the ones whose smallness, weakness and insignificance led the *Fascisti* to deem them unworthy of attack."

A law of December 30, 1926, gave sweeping powers over the coöperative movement to the Ministry of National Economy (later the Ministry of Corporations). At the same time, the *Ente Nazionale per la Cooperazione* was established, in place of an earlier Fascist coöperative league, to exercise general supervision over the societies in accordance with Fascist doctrines. Early in 1935 the *Ente* claimed the affiliation of 11,771 coöperative societies, with a membership of about 2,000,000. The former number includes 835 agricultural purchasing and selling coöperatives, with about 75,000 members

[18] Por, *Guilds and Co-operatives in Italy*, pp. 103-4.
[19] In *op. cit.*, p. 108.

and annual sales of some 1,120,000,000 lire; 2,763 coöperatives for processing farm commodities; 553 associations for agricultural credit and cattle insurance; and 399 farming coöperatives, cultivating about 115,000 hectares.[20] Thus coördinated and controlled, coöperation has been maintained and has even increased its membership and activities in certain fields. But the vitality of the coöperatives is much diminished by the utter dependence of the managers and directors on the government, and by their realization that all action on their part not in harmony with Fascist policy must quickly lead to trouble. Their behavior is circumspect and is likely to be guided by their desire to please political superiors rather than by a genuine concern for the welfare of the working masses. In consequence, the Italian coöperative movement—once characterized as "the most varied, fascinating and intellectually interesting in the evolution of economic democracy"[21] has lost all real contact with the workers and has become largely a device in the political and economic service of the government and the ruling class.

The middle-class character of coöperation under Fascism is most pronounced in agriculture. The leading members and chief beneficiaries of the coöperative marketing and processing societies are medium and big farmers.[22] This is also true of the

[20] Ministry of Corporations, *News Notes*, April 1935. For detailed (but uncritical) descriptions of co-operation under Fascism, see Walter, *Co-operation in Changing Italy;* Cotta, *Agricultural Co-operation in Fascist Italy;* Costanzo, "Agricultural Co-operation in Italy."

[21] Por, *Guilds and Co-operatives*, p. viii.

[22] For example, the dairy coöperatives had 240,000 members in 1935, and an annual output of 25 quintals (about 5,500 pounds) of milk per member; the coöperative wineries had 16,547 members in 1934, and annually processed 64.6 quintals (about 14,210 pounds) of grapes per member. These averages are far above the typical individual output of small peasants. Data from *Cooperazione Rurale*, December 1935.

"consortia for the defense of agricultural production"—associations of farmers for mutual help in combating plant diseases, maintaining quality standards and the like. For example, consortia have been established in particular regions to fix minimum standards for wines to be labeled as "typical" of such regions. But only the wealthier, better equipped vineyardists are able to meet these standards. The anti-phylloxera consortia operate similarly: the poorer peasants cannot afford to buy new vine stocks to take the place of old, diseased ones. Thus the consortia—in subtle ways—tend to eliminate the smaller peasants from the more profitable markets. Even in coöperation the curse of the poor is their poverty!

The coöperative farms—which at one time seemed capable, given sufficient encouragement, of significant contributions to the welfare of rural workers—have fared badly under the Fascist regime. In consequence of the decline of agricultural prices, the high rents, and the indifference of the government, the farm coöperatives have been declining steadily in recent years. As late as 1928 they cultivated nearly 250,000 hectares; by the end of 1935 they were reduced to 110,000 hectares.[23]

COMMODITY PRICE-SUPPORTING PROGRAMS

The class character of Fascist economic intervention is also reflected in the manner in which the government has attempted to relieve agriculture during the period of depression. The stabilization of the lira late in 1927 precipitated a decline in prices of farm products, which after 1928 was greatly intensified by the onset of world depression and a marked contraction in Italy's agricultural export markets. The consequent fall of prices, in the face of the heavy debt and tax bur-

[23] Acerbo, *La cooperazione agraria in Italia*, pp. 97-98; *Cooperazione Rurale*, December 1935.

dens of the agriculturists, made for widespread difficulties.[24] But by means of tariff protection, direct subsidies, organization of markets, and wage cutting, the government has done much to lighten the depression burdens of the propertied class and to shift them to the masses of small peasants and workers.

Tariff measures have been effective in supporting the prices of commodities on an import basis, such as wheat and sugar. The essence of the "Battle of Wheat" has been the imposition of extremely heavy duties on wheat imports. In consequence of this protective program, Italian consumers paid a premium on their wheat of roughly 32,000,000,000 lire during 1925-35.[25] But only the middle-class farmers and the large landowners have substantial supplies of marketable wheat, and therefore are in a position to profit from maintenance of domestic wheat prices. For the farm workers—as for all wage earners—the wheat tariff merely results in higher living costs.

The highly capitalistic sugar-beet industry has also been protected by very heavy duties on competitive imports.[26] Thus assured of a virtual monopoly of the domestic market, the Italian sugar producers have been in a position to maintain prices far above world levels, and to earn large profits.[27] But Italian sugar consumption—one of the lowest in the world,

[24] The total value of agricultural production is estimated to have fallen from 55,000,000,000 lire in 1926 to 25-30,000,000,000 in 1930. See Rota, "La crisi e l'agricoltura italiana."

[25] The import price of foreign wheat, less duty, declined approximately 60 per cent during 1928-35; the price of domestic non-durum wheat fell about 28 per cent in the same period. See pp. 67-68 above.

[26] An import duty on raw sugar, first class, of 165 lire per quintal was imposed on November 27, 1930; to this was added a duty of 15 per cent ad valorem on September 24, 1931. The 15 per cent duty was abolished on October 5, 1936; the specific duty on sugar was reduced to 132 lire per quintal on October 4, 1937.

[27] Although the price of Cuban sugar in London declined more than 50 per cent in the period 1929-35, Italian domestic wholesale sugar prices fell only about 8 per cent from 1929 to 1931, and remained practically stable

on a per capita basis—declined seriously during the depression.[28] In order to maintain prices, therefore, restriction of output was necessary. Beginning in 1931, the associations of beet producers and refiners, with governmental approval, have concluded agreements limiting acreage and production. In consequence, output has been curtailed, carryovers have been reduced and prices of beet-root, as well as refined, sugar have been well maintained.[29] Producers of tobacco have been in a similarly fortunate situation. The manufacture and sale of tobacco products is a government monopoly, and tobacco may be planted only under its authorization. Governmental control has led to the practical elimination of foreign competition in the Italian market, and in consequence it has been possible to maintain domestic prices of tobacco leaf well above the world level.[30]

---

during 1931-35. Prices of sugar beets have shown a similar stability. See International Institute of Agriculture, *International Yearbook of Agricultural Statistics, 1934-35;* Istituto Centrale di Statistica, *Annuario Statistico,* various years. Total net declared profits of the refining companies during the years of depression, 1928-33, ranged between 94,000,000 and 52,000,000 lire annually. See Associazione fra le Società Italiane per Azione, *Notizie Statistiche,* Vol. XIV, pp. 1527 ff.

[28] Total national consumption fell from 3,550,000 quintals in 1928 to 2,950,000 in 1934-35. See *Politica Sociale,* February-March 1936, p. 59. Per capita consumption in Italy in 1931 was 7.3 kilograms, as against 42.6 in the United States, 42.5 in England, 21.7 in France, 20.2 in Germany, 12.1 in Spain, and 9.3 in Poland. See Consorzio Nazionale Produttori Zucchero, *L'industria dello zucchero in Italia nel decennio 1924-33,* p. 17.

[29] The output of refined sugar in Italy in the seasons 1933-34 and 1934-35 was respectively, 32 and 21 per cent below that of 1929-30. Istituto Centrale di Statistica, *Annuario Statistico, 1936,* p. 67. See Rosenstock-Franck, *L'Économie corporative fasciste,* pp. 344-47; Fornaciari, *Attivitá e problemi dell'organizzazione dei bieticoltori;* Consorzio Nazionale Produttori Zucchero, *op. cit.*

[30] In 1931-33 the prices set by the monopoly were "probably 60-100 per cent higher than would be the delivered cost of Kentucky tobacco purchased from the United States." United States, 73d Congress, Letter from the Secretary of Agriculture: *World Trade Barriers in Relation to American Agriculture.*

More difficulty has been met in developing price-supports for farm products of which there are export surpluses, such as rice, silk, fruits, vegetables, wines. Such schemes as have been effected, however, exhibit a special concern for the commercial agriculturalists.

Rice cultivation is carried on predominantly by large-scale, capitalistic farm enterprise, employing many wageworkers. Only about half of the output is normally consumed in Italy, the remainder being exported. But world rice prices dropped drastically after 1929, and Italian producers, operating under high costs, found themselves in difficulties. The government undertook to aid them in a characteristic manner: an elaborate system of export dumping was developed behind the shelter of a heavy tariff on rice imports. The proceeds of marketing taxes, which ultimately must be paid by Italian rice consumers, have been used to subsidize exports and thus to maintain high domestic prices.[31]

[31] In October 1931, the *Ente Nazionale Rizi*, representing cultivators, millers, traders, and exporters, was formed under government auspices. This agency has attempted to fix minimum farm prices of rice, and has imposed a special duty payable by the first domestic producers. With the receipts from this tax it pays exporters a bounty, enabling them to sell abroad at the lower world prices. The chief burden of the tax is passed on in higher prices for the domestically consumed part of the crop. For details, see United States, 73d Congress, *World Trade Barriers*, pp. 417-20; International Institute of Agriculture, *The World Agricultural Situation, 1933-34*, pp. 325 ff.; Negri, *Le Riz en Italie*. Italian rice exports were sufficiently stimulated after devaluation of the lira in October 1936 to permit practical elimination of the bounty.

It is interesting to compare the course of world rice prices with those in Italy (average in July of each year in gold francs per quintal):

	1929	1930	1931	1932	1933	1934	1935
London, No. 2 Burma	33.5	28.6	17.8	14.2	11.8	10.7	11.6
Milan, Originario (white)	40.7	34.2	28.5	33.8	28.5	27.3	31.4

International Institute of Agriculture, *International Yearbook of Agricultural Statistics, 1934, 1934-35.*

The Italian silk, wine, orchard, and truck crops industries, too, have suffered severely in recent years in consequence of falling world prices and the intensified competition of foreign producers. Government intervention for support of the silk industry has consisted mainly of bounties to producers of mulberry leaves, silk-worm eggs, and cocoons, heavy subsidies to silk manufacturers and exporters, and reduction of textile-workers' wages.[32] Only by these means, apparently, has the industry been saved from collapse. With respect to fruits, vegetables, and wines (in the production of which both peasants and commercial agriculturists are engaged) depression relief has also taken the form of encouraging exports. The Italian methods of producing and marketing these commodities had lagged behind practices in competing countries, and it was believed that improvements might expand or at least maintain Italy's export markets. This task has been entrusted to the National Export Institute, organized in 1926 for the promotion of foreign trade in general. In recent years the Institute has attempted to rationalize the harvesting, grading, and packaging of an increasing number of farm products intended for export,[33] to extend the use of refrigeration, and to organize market information services. In order to raise quality, minimum standards have been prescribed, and only goods that meet such requirements may be exported. However desirable these developments are *per se*, in practice they tend to favor wealthy producers at the expense of the poor. Those

[32] See Giretti, "Il problema della seta in Italia," and "Un momento critico per la sete"; International Institute of Agriculture, *The World Agricultural Situation, 1933-34*.

[33] In 1934, citrus fruits, peaches, potatoes, cauliflower, tomatoes, rice, and wine were subject to such control. In March 1936, the National Export Institute became the National Fascist Institute for Foreign Exchange and was charged with general administration of the foreign-trade controls.

farmers who cannot afford to incur the expenses (of spraying, assorting, packaging, etc.) necessary to meet the minimum requirements are confined to the low-price domestic markets; thus the more profitable export opportunities are reserved for the medium-sized and large producers.[34]

Results of this special solicitude for the products of commercial and *latifondist* agriculture and relative neglect of peasant production are suggested by comparison of changes in the purchasing power of farm products in recent years.

TABLE 7

PURCHASING POWER OF IMPORTANT AGRICULTURAL COMMODITIES[35]

1930-34

Purchasing power in 1928 = 100

	1930	1932	1934		1930	1932	1934
Sugar beets	103	130	154	Corn	72	92	83
Sheep	129	113	135	Fresh deciduous fruits	87	78	80
Tobacco	101	106	120	Hemp	83	66	79
Wheat, durum	113	128	117	Wine	65	60	78
Olive oil	78	88	107	Tomatoes	117	92	74
Wheat, non-durum	111	119	105	Beans	91	73	60
Milk	103	104	109	Lemons	62	68	38
Rice	83	94	86	Silk cocoons	50	33	24
Oranges	69	105	84				

[34] Statistical confirmation of this is apparently not available. But Italian observers report that exports of fruits, vegetables, and wines from districts of small peasant cultivation have been declining seriously in recent years, whereas those from regions where big, commercial farming predominates have been maintained and in some cases even increased.

On the work of the National Export Institute and the situation of the fruit and vegetable industries, see M. Masi, "L'organizzazione commerciale per l'esportazione," in Ministero dell'Agricoltura e delle Foreste, *I progressi dell'agricoltura italiana in regime fascista*, pp. 335-44; Liebe, "Italiens Gartenbau"; International Institute of Agriculture, *The World Agricultural Situation, 1933-34*.

[35] Based on all-commodity wholesale-price index and commodity farm

It is significant that the purchasing power of commodities which are leading sources of income for the commercial farms of the North and of the great southern estates (such as sugar beets, sheep, tobacco, wheat, milk, rice) increased or at least remained stable during the depression. On the other hand, the purchasing power of products that are more important in providing cash incomes for peasants (such as wine, orchard, and truck crops) declined.[36]

CREDIT AND TAXATION

The agricultural price decline in recent years has of course intensified the pressure of debts on farmers and peasants. It is impossible to obtain precise data on the amount and distribution of agricultural debts, but observers agree that they are very heavy. Early in 1932 the Minister of Agriculture estimated the total at 8,500,000,000 lire, comprising 4,500,000,000 of mortgage debts, and 4,000,000,000 of short-term debts. According to other authorities the total was then even larger, exceeding 10,000,000,000 lire. Interest payments were estimated to absorb nearly a quarter of the total agricultural income.[37] Luigi Razza declared in 1934 that "three-

---

prices. Wholesale-price data from Istituto Centrale di Statistica, *Annuario Statistico, 1936*, p. 126; farm price data from Istituto Centrale di Statistica, *Indici dei prezzi.* In 1936, the purchasing power of some of these commodities was: durum wheat—120; non-durum wheat—113; olive oil—106; rice—110; corn—98; hemp—122; wine—40. Istituto Centrale di Statistica, *Annuario Statistico, 1937*, pp. 141-42, 148. Data on the other commodities are not available.

[36] This comparison would be more revealing if the agricultural production and marketing data were classified on the basis of sizes and types of farms. In the absence of such statistics, only rough generalizations can be made.

[37] But in particular regions, as in certain northern and central provinces where the amounts owed frequently surpass the value of the land itself, the burden is much heavier. See Mazzocchi-Alemanni, "I debiti dell'agricoltura."

quarters of the landowners are effectively in the hands of the banks and credit institutions." He pointed out that every landed proprietor must be considering the advisability of "lighting every hour a candle to Saint Benito [Mussolini] with the prayer that he might one fine day declare a general abrogation of their debts, or at least of their interest burden."[38]

In order to save the landowners—at any rate, the larger ones—from bankruptcy, recourse has been taken since early 1931 to various debt-lightening measures (such as loans at low interest rates to wheatgrowers and "agriculturists of special merit," extension of the period in which private reclamation obligations must be met, increased participation by the government in interest payments, reduction of interest rates, conversion of obligations), which of course represent further governmental subventions.[39] But apparently the big landowners have been the chief beneficiaries. According to a writer in *Agricoltura Fascista* (April 29, 1935) not less than 90 per cent of the landowners aided by these special measures were *latifondisti* and agricultural companies. The small landowners have received almost no help; thousands of requests for financial aid have been left unanswered by the Ministry of Agriculture. The suggestion is also made by this writer that certain persons close to the government have been granted inordinate favors. On the other hand, observes the *Lavoro Fascista* of August 30, 1936, "the great majority of rural wage-workers are frequently obliged by the needs of their families to borrow from local shopkeepers at not exactly philanthropic rates of interest."

Moreover, increasing control by the government and the

[38] R. Accademia dei Georgofili," Convegno per la bonifica integrale," pp. 366-67.

[39] For details, see Costanzo, "System of Agricultural Credit in Italy."

large financial institutions over the rural banks[40] has operated to reduce the borrowing ability of small peasants. The less localized the management of the credit agencies, the less is known about the personality of the would-be borrower and the more necessary it is to insist on security in real property. But many small peasants, not having sufficient property, thus find it impossible to borrow from the banks, and so must turn to private moneylenders, rich farmers and landlords. Usurious interest rates—in some cases ranging as high as 50 to 100 per cent per year—must be paid for such loans.[41]

The Fascist regime shows a similar discrimination between the propertied and unpropertied in its taxation policy. The 1919 program of the Fascists announced, among other things: "We demand: (a) a heavy extraordinary tax on capital . . . with a view to its partial expropriation; (b) the seizure of all the property of religious associations . . . ; (c) revision of all war-supplies contracts and seizure of 85 per cent of the war-time super-profits. . . ."[42] But a month after the "March on Rome" De' Stefani—Minister of Finance in Mussolini's first cabinet—declared that "a financial policy based on the persecution of capital is infected with madness."[43] Thereafter, nothing more was heard of the proposed capital levy, of confiscation of church property and war profits. Instead, capital issues were freed from taxation (November 10, 1922), the official commission of inquiry that had been charged with discovering illicit profits on war-supplies contracts was dissolved and its findings were suppressed (November 19, 1922), the inherit-

[40] Developed under a series of laws beginning in July 1927.

[41] For outlines of the agricultural credit reforms of the Fascists, see Costanzo, *op. cit.*; Hazen, "Agricultural Credit in Italy."

[42] *Popolo d'Italia*, April 20, 1920.

[43] See Perroux, *Contribution à l'étude de l'économie et des finances publiques de l'Italie depuis la guerre*, pp. 211 ff.

ance tax was abolished (August 20, 1923). And finally the government undertook to pay the Holy See 1,750,000,000 lire as damages for the occupation of Rome in 1870 (June 11, 1929).

The Fascists insist that a "policy aimed at increased production" (*concetto produttivistico*) has guided their taxation policy—that they have wished to sustain capital, not capitalism. Yet, at any rate so far as agriculture is concerned, it is not so much the real producers as the absentee proprietors who have been protected. For example, on January 4, 1923, a new tax on agricultural income was introduced. This provided that, in the case of proprietors whose land is cultivated by wageworkers or share-tenants, the tax would be based on income remaining *after* payment of wages or crop shares; but in the case of non-employing cultivators, it would be based on income *including* imputed wages. It is estimated that the effect of this distinction is to make the income-tax burden of small, independent peasant proprietors double that of absentee landlords.[44] Again, a revision of the cadastral survey was ordered on January 7, 1923, to determine the extent and value of each farm and estate as a basis for the land tax. Critics declare that this revision was made under the influence of big landowners and resulted in a marked undervaluation of large estates and overvaluation of peasant property.[45]

To be sure, the tax outlays of all classes have been rising since the advent of Fascism. It is estimated that the total tax burden rose from 12.5 per cent of the national income in 1913-14 to 20 per cent in 1925-26 and 29-32 per cent in 1932-34,

[44] See Nicoletti, *Le Fascisme contre le paysan*, pp. 65 ff.; Marabini, "La mezzadria in Italia," p. 219.

[45] Silone, *Der Fascismus*, p. 163. For an estimate of the direct and indirect tax burden borne by agriculture, see Confederazione Nazionale Fascista degli Agricoltori, *Dieci anni di attività sindacale, 1922-32.*

thus becoming one of the heaviest in the world.[46] The middle class in towns and country is now staggering under the weight of taxation. But the low-income groups seem to have borne more than their proportionate share of this increase. Taxation of income begins at 2,000 lire per year, thus reaching down into the ranks of the working population. And indirect taxes have risen markedly. For example, receipts from manufacturing taxes on sugar, wine, etc., from the charges of the state tobacco and salt monopolies, and from customs duties expanded as follows, in billions of lire: fiscal years, *1919-23*, 15.7; *1923-27*, 22.4; *1927-31*, 30.0; *1931-35*, 26.9.[47]

Thus, "the government has one very long arm and one very short one. The long one is for taking, and reaches everywhere, and the short one is for giving, but it only reaches those who are nearest."[48]

THE AGRICULTURAL "CORPORATIONS"

Fascist spokesmen and sympathizers view the long-heralded establishment of "category corporations," early in 1934, as completing the structure of the syndical and corporative sys-

[46] Mortara, *Prospettive Economiche, 1929, 1933, 1934, passim.* Mortara estimates the tax burden in 1929 as 25 per cent of the total private income, as against 23 per cent in England and France, and 20 per cent in Germany.

[47] Istituto Centrale di Statistica, *Annuario Statistico, 1936*, p. 173. These receipts constituted 22 per cent of the total government revenues in the fiscal years 1919-23, 27 per cent in 1923-27, 37 per cent in 1927-31, and 36 per cent in 1931-35. In terms of gold lire the total indirect tax revenue was 110 per cent greater in 1929-30 than in 1913-14. Ministero delle Finanze, *Il bilancio dello Stato dal 1913-14 al 1929-30*, p. 96. The general level of tariff rates (in terms of 1914 gold lire) in 1933 was estimated to be 185 per cent above that in 1914 and 44 per cent above that in 1921; allowing for the decline of prices, it was 274 per cent above that in 1914 and 140 per cent above that in 1921. See Répaci, "La misura delle variazione delle tariffe doganale."

[48] Silone, *Bread and Wine* (Harper and Brothers, New York, 1937), p. 285. Reprinted by permission of the publishers.

tem, effecting an economy in which individual interests are subordinated to collective interests, and perhaps even beginning a type of planned economy.[49] It is therefore important to consider the nature of these new organs, and their significance in terms of agricultural enterprise and the welfare of the rural population.

Mussolini defines the corporations as "the instrument which, under the aegis of the State, carries out completely, organically and in the general interest, the regulation of the productive forces, with a view to the development of the wealth, the political power and the well-being of the Italian people."[50] The corporations are expected to advise the government on economic problems, to conciliate labor disputes, and to make recommendations to the responsible authorities for measures concerning working conditions and the production and distribution of commodities. They are grouped as follows: (1) eight corporations relating to all the stages of production, processing, and marketing of agricultural commodities; (2) eight corporations relating to the production and marketing of non-agricultural commodities; (3) six corporations relating

[49] "The law of April, 1926, regarding syndical organization envisaged the eventual establishment of corporations, which were to serve as liaison organs between employers' and workers' organizations in each category. No steps toward the creation of these corporations were taken at first, and the functions they were intended to perform were temporarily entrusted in 1931 to the National Council of Corporations which had been established in the previous year. This council . . . is designed to act as a coordinating and consulting body, charged with the task of achieving unity in national production. . . . Actually, however, all important measures on economic, financial and social matters have emanated from the political organs of the government." Dean, "The Economic Situation in Italy: The Corporative System," p. 300. Finally it was decided to complete the "corporative" system. After legislative preliminaries, Mussolini announced, on May 9, 1934, the formation of 22 corporations representing the various branches of the economy.

[50] See Costanzo, "Corporative Organization in Italy."

to the production of services. The first group, which is of particular interest here, includes the corporations for cereals; fruits, vegetables, and flowers; grapes and wine; beets and sugar; olives and olive oil; animal husbandry and fishing; forestry, lumber, and wood products; textile fibers and products. Each corporation is headed by a council, composed of delegates of the Fascist party, representatives of the employers' and workers' syndicates in the industries concerned, and technical experts—all appointed, directly or indirectly, by the government.[51] According to Salvemini, "almost all the most important Italian capitalists" are to be found among the 268 employer representatives in the corporation councils. "Among the (268) persons who were supposed to represent the employees there were 127 lawyers, professors, doctors, engineers, accountants, etc. Of men who really came from the rank and file there were scarcely twenty."[52] These councils merely recommend action to the government; their proposals are effected only when approved by a Central Corporative Committee and the "Head of the Government."[53]

[51] The council of the Cereals Corporation, for example, comprises a chairman (Mussolini) and "three representatives of the Fascist National Party; seven representatives of the employers and seven of the workers engaged in the production of cereals; one representative of the employers and one of the workers engaged in the threshing industry; three representatives of the employers and three of the workers engaged in the milling industry, in the rice industry, the confectionery industry, and the alimentary pastes industries; one representative of the employers and one of the workers engaged in the baking industry; three representatives of the employers and three of the workers engaged in the grain trade and in the trade in the other products above enumerated; one representative of the consumers' cooperative societies; one representative of the agricultural experts belonging to the liberal professions; one representative of the artisans." Costanzo, *op. cit.*

[52] In *Under the Axe of Fascism*, p. 122.

[53] For details of the structure, and functioning of the corporations see Costanzo, *op. cit.;* Salvemini, *op. cit.*, pp. 110-32.

Nearly three years have passed since the corporations were established. In this period, the councils of the eight agricultural corporations have met at least once and have made numerous recommendations for governmental action. It is not too early, then, to ask how they have been concerned with "the regulation of productive forces."

Examination of the agenda and resolutions of these corporations shows that their interests, programs, and powers are essentially those of chambers of commerce, trade associations, and legislative lobbies. Their recommendations almost exclusively seek limitation of competitive imports, subsidization of marketing schemes, restriction of output, support for price-control devices—the stock in trade of monopoly-minded enterprisers. With respect to social and economic problems of any fundamental, general importance their interest and authority have been extremely slight. For example, the Cereals Corporation (in its meeting beginning September 28, 1935) recommended: (1) development of methods of reducing seasonal fluctuations in grain prices; (2) limits to the extension of milling capacity; (3) fixing of retail bread prices by syndical and political organizations; (4) restriction of retail bread dealers' sources of supply; (5) prohibition of retail bread sales by itinerant vendors in towns of more than 5,000 inhabitants; (6) restriction of the number of rice mills; (7) fixing of terms for the hire of threshing machines. Representative proposals made by the other agricultural corporations were for a reduction of oil-seed imports, development of a scheme for removing burdensome surpluses of wine by converting wine into alcohol, wider use of Italian motors in fishing vessels, tariff protection for the tuna industry, increased use of alcohol as a motor fuel, regulation of wholesale and retail sugar prices, further support for exports of fruits and vegetables, higher duties on lumber imports, development of uniform-quality marks for cheeses, tariff support for the castor-oil industry. Only one of the many recommendations was at all concerned with the conditions of workers: a proposal by the Animal Husbandry and Fisheries Corporation for the extension of social insurance benefits to fishermen (so far, this proposal has not received governmental approval).[54] One searches in vain for any suggestions for raising mass living levels, for rationalizing productive and distributive methods in order to make goods available in larger quantities at lower prices, for controlling quality and prices in the interests of worker-consumers.[55] Of social-economic planning, even in its most limited sense, there is not a trace. Requests for more government intervention in the interests of the propertied class—translated into the jargon of "national welfare," "class collaboration" and "corporative economy," and punctuated with obeisances to the Fascist regime—this is all that one finds in the record of the corporations.

Certainly in Italy, as elsewhere, the government in recent years has come to intervene more and more in the affairs of

[54] Data from Ministry of Corporations, *News Notes*, 1935-36; *Sindacato e Corporazione*, January-November 1935; "Le corporazione all'opera," in *Politica Sociale*, February-March 1936; Costanzo, *op. cit.;* Confederazione Fascista dei Lavoratori dell'Agricoltura, *Il lavoro agricolo nelle attività delle corporazioni.*

[55] Gino Arias, a leading exponent of "corporative" economics, points out why the corporations must not be considered agencies in the development of economic planning: "One must first and foremost exclude the State or any public body such as a syndicate, or more important still a corporation, from taking upon itself the management of enterprises and thus excluding private enterprise or placing it in a thoroughly subordinate position. This would be in contradiction to the Charter of Labor. The discipline of economic relations entrusted to the syndicates and corporations is not planned to exclude competition by the establishment of open or masked monopolies. This would be the new path to socialism." *Popolo d'Italia,* April 18, 1933, quoted by Elwin, *Fascism at Work,* p. 193.

agriculture. Fascist intervention, however, helps the propertied class and the hierarchy of officials and Blackshirts, not the rural masses. It is the big industrialists, great landlords, and commercial agriculturists who find championship in the actions—if not the speeches—of the Fascists. It is they who have been maintained and even strengthened by encouragement of monopolistic practices and by special subventions. And the only socialization has been that of business losses.

VIII: The Discipline of Poverty

After all this suffering and all this fighting, all these tears and all this anguish, all this blood, all this hate, and all this hopelessness, What must we do?

—IGNAZIO SILONE[1]

THE demagogues attempt to identify the goals of Fascism with the welfare of workers and peasants. But Fascist policy operates in the interests of absentee landownership, commercialized agriculture, monopolistic finance capital. For the millions of poor peasants and agricultural workers the masquerade of "deproletarization" and "ruralization" means subjection to the bureaucracy and the propertied groups.

The Fascist era has seen a decline of small peasant proprietorship, deterioration of the contractual status of share-tenants, enclosure of common lands. The "Battle of Wheat" and the land reclamation program, perhaps the most widely publicized economic undertakings of Fascism, serve predominantly the propertied class. Rural coöperation has become business-minded. During the period of world depression, the Fascist government has taken vigorous steps—in the form of commodity price-supporting programs, control of credit, and levying of taxes—to lighten the burdens of the absentee owners and to shift them to the rural masses. The corporative organization, professedly a means of subordinating individual interests to the broad necessities of the community, in practice is a device for further government intervention in the interests of property rights. The militant workers' movement

[1] *Fontamara* (Random House, Inc., New York, 1934). Reprinted by permission of the publishers.

has been shattered, and many of the gains in working conditions achieved by it have been lost. The autocratic syndicate system is essentially an instrument of mass control in the hands of a political party serving the vested interests of bureaucracy and great landed and industrial property. The eight-hour day in agriculture is forgotten, real wages have been forced down to miserable subsistence levels, the uncertainty of employment has increased seriously. Prospects of becoming independent farmers, at home or abroad, have dimmed. Instead, there is developing a relationship to the soil that is uncomfortably close to serfdom.

The deterioration of working conditions during the fifteen years of Fascist rule is reflected in a marked decline of mass living levels.

The total agricultural net income in 1928—a year of relative prosperity—is estimated to have been 30,000,000,000 lire, as against a total national income of 94,000,000,000 lire.[2] Since 48 per cent of the agricultural income was remuneration for capital and enterprise, going mainly to landlords and large commercial farmers, the remaining 52 per cent constituted labor income. That is, the working rural population—almost half of the country's entire population—received scarcely a sixth of the national income.

Italian income data are meager and uncertain. No estimates of national income and its distribution in the years since 1928 are available. But it is certain that agricultural income fell markedly in the period 1928-35. Average prices of farm commodities in 1934 were 44 per cent below their level in 1928.

[2] The real per capita national income was about 12 per cent below that of 1914. Meliadò, "Il reddito privato degli italiani nel 1928"; McGuire, *Italy's International Economic Position*, p. 447. See also, De Vita, "Il reddito dell'Italia al 1928."

And farm production, as a whole, expanded relatively little in this period. However, average prices of production goods and services purchased by farmers and peasants declined only 29 per cent.[3] Living costs, too, fell less rapidly than farm prices. Taxes, rents and interest declined even more slowly. The brunt of the price decline seems to have been borne by the products of small farmers and peasants.[4] These observations, rough approximations as they must be, together with data on the fall of rural wages,[5] point to a severe reduction during recent years in the real income of the agricultural masses.[6]

More concrete evidence of growing poverty is provided by *food consumption* data. At best, the diet of the Italian working population—urban and rural—has been inadequate.[7] But since 1930 both the quantity and quality of food available per capita have fallen appreciably. Most serious is the reduced consumption of wheat, meats, sugar, and fats. In fact, average wheat consumption is now lower than immediately before the War. A sharp drop in the use of salt suggests that less cooked food is being eaten.[8] The per capita daily food ration, in cal-

[3] Istituto Centrale di Statistica, *Indici dei prezzi*, pp. 16-19.

[4] See above, pp. 143-49.

[5] See above, pp. 110-18.

[6] For further data in respect of rural income, see Franciosa, "Bilanci e consumi delle famiglie agricole," and the studies of peasant family living standards, Istituto Nazionale di Economia Agraria, *Monografie di famiglie rurali.*

[7] In 1924 the per capita food ration in Italy appeared to be "notably less than before the war. The ration was deficient not only in the total number of calories, but also in the quality of its ingredients, which contain an insufficient quantity of fats and proteins. . . . The indices of food consumption prove that the Italian people, who, even before the war were not abundantly nourished from the physiological standpoint, have been compelled to reduce still further their consumption of food." C. Gini, "The Present Economic Status of Italy," in McGuire, *op. cit.*, pp. 513-15.

[8] "For the carnivorous rich, salt is a luxury; for the herbivorous pro-

ories, is estimated to have dropped as follows: *1922*, 3,141; *1926-30*, 2,917; *1929-33*, 2,892; *1933*, 2,790.[9]

TABLE 8

IMPORTANT FOODS AVAILABLE FOR CONSUMPTION[10]

1926-1936

Average kilograms or liters per year per capita

	1926-30	1931-35	1936
Wheat flour, kg.	142.5	125.7	118.6
Potatoes, kg.	35.4	35.9	29.6
Corn flour, kg.	27.6	25.6	24.2
Rice, kg.	6.2	6.2	7.1
Beans, kg.	5.0	5.0	4.0
Meats, kg.	18.8	16.4	16.1
Eggs, kg.	6.3	6.7	6.6
Cheese, kg.	4.6	4.9	4.3
Olive oil, liters	6.1	5.2	5.1
Butter and lard, kg.	5.1	4.8	4.8
Sugar, kg.	9.1	7.2	6.7
Milk, liters	33.1	33.9	32.8
Fruits, vegetables and greens, kg.	123.2	108.8	100.1
Salt, kg.	8.0	7.1	6.9

These data of course refer to *national* average consumption, the consumption of rich and poor alike. No quantitative information on the food standards of the rural population as a

---

letariat of Italy it is a necessity." F. Flora, *Manuale della scienza delle finanze* (Leghorn, 1927), p. 170, quoted by Salvemini, *Under the Axe of Fascism*, p. 359.

[9] McGuire, *op. cit.;* Bottazzi, Niceforo, and Quagliariello, *Documenti per lo studio della alimentazione della popolazione italiana nell'ultimo cinquantennio*, p. 215; Istituto Centrale di Statistica, *Annuario Statistico*, *1935*, p. 164; *1936*, p. 139.

[10] Istituto Centrale di Statistica, *Annuario Statistico*, *1936*, p. 139; *1937*, p. 163. See the 1935 *Annuario* (p. 164) for another picture of recent consumption trends.

It may be noted that sales of tobacco products fell about 20 per cent in 1928-35, and retail sales of clothing and furniture declined about 30 per cent in 1929-34. *Annuario Statistico*, *1935*, p. 165; *1936*, p. 140.

whole, but only summary qualitative description, is available. For example, the Fascist Confederation of Agricultural Workers in 1930 published a report on rural living conditions, in which appears the following generalization about the food habits of the peasantry:

. . . In North and Central Italy, where agriculture is more progressive, the peasant is able to enjoy a greater variety of foodstuffs than elsewhere. *Polenta* [corn meal mush], pastes, greens, vegetables, fruit, milk, cheese, pork sausages, constitute the Northern peasant's rations. . . . Fresh meat is eaten once, at most twice, a week. . . . In the South, however, the peasant's diet is more frugal and simple. Bread, pastes, vegetables, fruit, olive oil, are the basic diet. Dried and pickled fish are eaten during the winter, while meat is almost unknown—at the most only on feast days. The diet of the day wage laborers is worse everywhere.[11]

An Italian expert in nutrition (and a Fascist sympathizer) in 1930 described the trend in rural food consumption:

Towards the end of the nineteenth and in the early part of the twentieth century . . . the agricultural workers made notable advances in their wage scales and were able to obtain higher standards of living and to render their food more varied. A fine and encouraging advance in civilization, to which was put the characteristic seal: the rapid decrease of pellagra. . . . Whoever is acquainted with country life knows that the peasants continued after the War to live better than formerly, and that their food continued quite good. Our peasant learned, while continuing to use maize, to consume good wheat bread, eggs, milk, and dairy products, sugar and meat. His diet remained frugal, but meat was no more what it had once been, a purely luxury food, reserved for some rare feast day. The peasant ate better, and pellagra disappeared almost entirely. . . . But this phenomenon, being quite recent, could not possess the characteristics of absolute stability. It was a state of equilibrium, for obvious reasons unstable. . . . *Mal-*

[11] Confederazione Nazionale dei Sindacati Facista dell'Agricoltura, *Indagine sulle condizioni di vita dei contadini*, pp. 463 ff.

nutrition, by many held to have gone forever, returns in wide areas to the disadvantage of the peasant. . . . Wherever the peasant has to go back to the poor, monotonous diet of former times based on nothing, or almost nothing, but maize, it is certain that he will again fall victim to pellagra. Those who are in places of command will do well to keep their eyes open.[12]

Now, observers report increasing consumption of *polenta* in recent years among the peasants and farm workers (including those in the South, where formerly it was almost unknown). But this tendency is even to be encouraged, according to a Fascist agricultural expert, who points out that

the agrarian crisis will be overcome by producing more and at lower prices, and at the same time by living, at least for several years, very parsimoniously, that is, by spending as little as possible on food and clothing. *Polenta* must again return to its pristine honor. If to maize we add beans, we will have the two principal foods, which will be supplemented by potatoes and vegetables. Little bread and less meat. I see no other way out of the present difficult situation.[13]

The national food consumption data at least suggest the exceedingly low standards of Italian workers. They also indicate that the decline in workers' incomes under Fascism has been reflected in a lowering of essential consumption. (This seems to imply that even in the immediate post-War years, when real wages reached the highest levels recorded, the Italian workers could not have been much above a bare subsistence level.) However, the former Undersecretary of Cor-

[12] Messedaglia, "L'alimentazione dei contadini," *Atti dell'Accademia di Agricoltura, Scienze e Lettere di Verona*, Serie V, Vol. VII (Verona, 1930), p. 22 ff., quoted by Salvemini, *Under the Axe of Fascism*, p. 360. Italics by C. T. S.

[13] Professor Bizozzero in the *Corriere Padano*, June 14, 1931, quoted by Salvemini, *op. cit.*, p. 359.

porations, Giuseppe Bottai, has discovered real virtues in the decline of wages—it "would have valuable psychological and moral consequences by enforcing a more rigorous way of living."[14]

However, Fascist leaders sometimes concede that food consumption standards are hardly satisfactory. Thus "in 1929 Mussolini admitted that there are communes in Sardinia and South Italy where for months at a time the inhabitants have to live on wild plants."[15] Speaking in the Chamber of Deputies in 1929, the deputy Zingali pointed out that "the daily per capita food ration in Italy amounts to 3,100 calories, that is, 200 calories less than the physiologists consider necessary for the adult. Our ration is perhaps the lowest in all Europe."[16] Nevertheless, in the following year Mussolini declared: "Fortunately the Italian people is not yet accustomed to eating several times a day, and, having a modest level of living, feels less deficiency and suffering."[17]

Housing and sanitary conditions, too, are deplorable in many districts. According to a survey made by the Fascist Confederation of Agricultural Workers, the total number of rural houses in 1933 was 3,479,200. Of these 276,810 were judged to be "in conditions of almost absolute uninhabitability" such as would warrant their being demolished. Another 739,580 were also "almost uninhabitable," but possibly could be made satisfactory by "major repairs." Not less than 6,500,000 persons (a third of the rural population) were living in these houses.[18] According to the Istituto Centrale di Statistica, 55,285

[14] *Sole*, January 1, 1931.

[15] Seldes, *Sawdust Caesar*, p. 289.

[16] Parlamento Italiano, *Atti*, Camera dei Deputati, XXVIII Legislatura: *Discussioni, 28 novembre 1929-9 aprile 1930*, p. 1393.

[17] *Corriere della Sera*, December 19, 1930.

[18] Confederazione Fascista dei Lavoratori dell'Agricoltura, *Per le case rurali.*

rural habitations in 1933 were made of earth and foliage, and 6,397 were caves.[19] At least 350,000-450,000 peasants lived in these hovels.

The following excerpts from the report of the Agricultural-Workers' Confederation[20] describe more eloquently than statistics can the living conditions of peasants and rural workers throughout the country:

Piedmont

Alessandria: The old houses are hygienically defective, the air is bad, and the rooms are crowded; frequently the peasants live in the stables during the winter.

Lombardy

Brescia: The rural houses generally are inadequate. The wage-workers' families, in order to pay the rent demanded, must adapt themselves to living in one, at most two, rooms. . . .

Cremona: The farm proprietors are not interested in the tenants' houses, and those who manage the big farms themselves bother only about improvement and modernization of stables, barns, etc. . . .

Venetia

Venezia: Farm workers are still living in old wooden barracks built during the War. . . .

[19] Istituto Centrale di Statistica, *Indagine sulle case rurali in Italia*. This report gives a less unfavorable picture of the rural housing situation than does that of the Agricultural-Workers' Confederation. Only 4 per cent of the houses were found to warrant demolition, 14 per cent required "major repairs," and 28 per cent needed "minor repairs." See the Istituto's *Indagine sulle abitazioni al 21 aprile 1931*, Part 2, for detailed data on general housing conditions.

[20] Confederazione Fascista dei Lavoratori dell'Agricoltura, *Per le case rurali*, pp. 37-51. These descriptions differ little from those given by the parliamentary commission of inquiry in its report of 1909-11. See Faina, *Inchiesta parlamentare*.

Rovigo: Many peasants inhabit one-room houses made of cane and straw. . . .

Emilia

Modena: The houses inhabited by small proprietors and tenants are built generally for the needs of agriculture rather than for the needs of their families. . . .

Piacenza: Everywhere one sees overcrowding and promiscuity. . . .

Tuscany

Lucca: Nearly all the houses are without adequate water supply, lack latrines, and are badly neglected.

Latium

Rieti: Eighty per cent of the houses do not meet the most modest needs of the tenant families. . . .

Campania

Avellini: . . . Rural houses are made of tree trunks and corn stalks. In many parts of the country the workers live in caves dug out of the rock. . . .

Apulia

Bari: The rural population normally lives in the big towns . . . in generally unhygienic houses. Sometimes a big family lives in one room, together with the work animals.

Lucania

Matera: Many of the habitations are caves, into which air and light come only through the entrance.

Potenza: In the towns many peasants live below the street level, in damp, dark and stuffy cellars. . . . In the country most of the houses are made of straw, stones, and mud. The family and its animals live in one room without flooring or windows.

Sicily

Agrigento: One room, lacking ventilation, light, and flooring, and often without water, is the usual habitation of rural families in the towns. . . . The peasants sleep, often in deplorable promiscuity, on straw mattresses supported by trestles alongside the mangers of the animals. . . .

Catania: Latrines are almost completely unknown to the peasants; their standards of cleanliness leave much to be desired. . . .

Sardinia

Nuoro: The houses frequently have no windows and no flooring. . . . Animals and people live together. . . .

Mussolini himself has fittingly described the situation thus: "In many European countries, and also in Italy, the rural housing conditions are absolutely deplorable. They are very crowded and lack the most primitive hygienic conveniences. The young peasant, who during his years of military service has seen the houses of the city, makes comparisons and does not adapt himself easily to his old home."[21] But he paints a more attractive picture of the peasant houses of the Fascist future: "The order of the day is this: Within a few decades all peasants and farm workers must possess large, healthful houses, in which the rural generations can live through the centuries, in which the race will find a secure foundation. Only thus is it possible to combat the poisons of urbanism, only thus is it possible to bring back to the villages and fields the deluded peasants who have followed the urban mirage of money wages and easy diversions."[22]

So far, however, little has been done toward the fulfillment of this promise. A few thousand peasants have been settled in new houses in the reclaimed areas, particularly in the Agro

[21] *Popolo d'Italia*, July 3, 1933.

[22] Istituto Centrale di Statistica, *Indagine sulle case rurali*, p. 7.

Pontino, the official show place. Total expenditures, governmental and private, for rural housing amounted to but 285,000,000 lire in the fiscal years 1929-35, that is, hardly 5 per cent of the total land reclamation outlays. Nor are landowners placed by the collective contracts under any significant obligations to provide decent housing for their farm workers and tenants.

Admittedly, the task outlined by the Duce would be very costly. According to an agricultural expert, 13,500,000,000 to 21,500,000,000 lire over a period of thirty years would be needed, the government providing at least half.[23] The dictatorship has, however, found billions for public buildings and monuments, for armaments and imperialistic adventures.

On the other hand, the enlarged reclamation program of the Fascists has contributed to the improvement of *rural health* by diminishing the breeding places of malarial mosquitoes. The number of deaths attributed to malaria has declined enormously since the beginning of this century. Per million inhabitants, it was 416 in 1902, 76 in 1912, 111 in 1922, and 40 in 1935. But morbidity rates are more significant as an index of the extent of the disease. The number of malaria cases reported per million inhabitants was 5,442 in 1902, 4,768 in 1912, 6,417 in 1922, and 3,823 in 1935. The average number of cases in 1933-35 was actually above that in 1912-14.[24]

[23] Mazzocchi-Alemanni, "Le case rurali." This author also becomes rhapsodic when he contemplates the future: "It will be a generation of new peasants, who will see the old rural housing problem solved, who will live with new vigor in large, hygienic houses, blessing the Man who, after thirty centuries, has raised the rural masses to first place in the national policy."

[24] Data from Ministero del Interno, Direzione Generale della Sanità Pubblica. In particular regions the malarial death rate is still high. In 1934 the number of deaths from malaria per million inhabitants ranged between 200 and 300 in South Italy, reaching 300 in Sicily and Sardinia,

This suggests that the disease is still much more widespread than Fascist commentators, who usually point only to mortality rates, admit. It may also imply that measures for curing malaria cases (as with quinine treatment) have been more successful than those for reducing the breeding grounds of the Anopheles mosquitoes (as by drainage of marshes).

The incidence of other diseases—such as typhoid fever, cholera, tuberculosis, pellagra—to which the rural population formerly was especially subject has also been much reduced during the past thirty or forty years. Another index of improving general health is the decline in the death rate. The number of deaths per thousand men fell from 29.2 in 1880-92 to 20.4 in 1910-12, 18.3 in 1920-22, 15.3 in 1930-32. Mortality of infants aged less than one year was 219.1 per thousand in 1872-75; 142 in 1910-12; 128.8 in 1920-22; and 109.6 in 1930-32.[25] These declines are a reflection of long-run improvement of living conditions and developments in public hygiene and medicine. There is no reason to assume that the Fascist regime *per se* has contributed to advances in health that have been so long under way.[26] Indeed, it is much more likely that the regime will bear responsibility (at some time in the future) for an abrupt rise in the death rate.

The general level of *education*—as measured by school attendance, ability to read, and the like—has been rising fairly steadily during the last two or three generations. In 1861 only 25 per cent of the population over the age of six could read. By 1901 the percentage had risen to 52, by 1911 to 62, by

---

and was between 200 and 250 in Latium, Venetia, Lombardy, and Emilia. Istituto Centrale di Statistica, *Annuario Statistico, 1935*, p. 32.

[25] *Ibid.*, pp. 21, 30.

[26] Some observers fear a recurrence of pellagra, which had well-nigh disappeared, in view of the decline of dietary standards in recent years.

1921 to 73, and by 1931 to 79. The *Mezzogiorno* lags behind the rest of Italy: in 1931 the percentage of illiterates in the population more than six years of age was 8 in North Italy, 21 in Central Italy, and 39 in South Italy. In the country as a whole, 30 per cent of the persons occupied in agriculture were unable to read, as against 14 per cent in transportation, 9 per cent in industry, and 8 per cent in commerce. But in the South more than 53 per cent of the rural workers and peasants were illiterate.[27]

Thus, although schooling in the rural districts is more adequate than a generation ago, it is still not highly effective. The government is spending considerably more on education than in the past,[28] and school attendance is formally required, at least in the cities, of all children between the ages of six and fourteen. Yet many peasant children get little education. Data on attendance are more significant as to the effectiveness of the schools than are rates of illiteracy. In 1935-36 the number of children required to attend elementary public schools was 5,261,320, but only 4,719,573 were actually registered; 4,137,380 were examined, and 3,087,590 were promoted. That is, more than half a million children did not attend (many because they were needed for work, or because their parents were too poor to provide them with adequate clothing), and of those enrolled in the schools, nearly 600,000 were so irregular in attendance as to preclude them from examination. Again the highly agricultural South falls behind; of the Southern

[27] Istituto Centrale di Statistica, *Censimento generale della popolazione . . . 21 aprile 1931*, Vol. IV.

[28] Since 1926 about twice as much per capita (in terms of 1914 gold lire) as immediately before the World War. This comparison, however, is not accurate, inasmuch as expenditures formerly included in local government budgets now are comprised in the budget of the national government.

children obliged to attend, 16 per cent were in fact not registered, and 15 per cent of those in attendance were not examined.[29]

The schools, as well as the youth organizations and the workers' recreational associations, are powerful instruments for the dissemination of Fascist propaganda. The government, of course, controls all formal means of communication and information, and makes full use of them to maintain and strengthen its authority and prestige. Newspapers are directed to emphasize particular news items and to speak softly or not at all about others.[30] (A number of agricultural newspapers and periodicals, too, are directly subsidized by the government.) Every possible occasion is seized upon for propaganda purposes. Workers' old-age pension certificates are distributed with official flourish; a special order—the Stella al Merito Rurale—has been created for bestowal on persons who have rendered conspicuous service to agriculture; premiums and

[29] Istituto Centrale di Statistica, *Annuario Statistico, 1937*, p. 261.

[30] Thus, the government press instructions of July 7, 1932, ordered newspaper articles "on the return to the land, calling attention to how the régime has since 1922 made an eminently rural policy." Seldes, *Sawdust Caesar*, p. 317.

The radio and films, especially newsreels, are employed similarly. A government-controlled institution, the *Ente Radio Rurale*, has been organized for the purpose of reaching the rural population by means of the radio. The *Ente* promotes broadcasts of technical and general interest to farmers and peasants and has standardized a low-price receiving set suited for use in rural districts. Many rural schools have been provided with receivers. See Dusmet, "Spare Time Organizations for Agricultural Workers in Italy."

In mid-1935 the Italian radio stations broadcasted "the first educational program of the *Ente Radio Rurale*. The Vice-secretary of the U.F.G., on behalf of the Secretary of the Party and the President of the *Ente*, commanded all scholars of Italy to salute the Duce, after which a talk was broadcast on 'A visit to a camp of Blackshirts preparing to leave for East Africa.'" Ministry of Corporations, *News Notes*, October 1935.

prizes are given to parents of many children and to peasant families long established on a particular farm. It is constantly suggested that the history of modern Italy before the "March on Rome" is ignoble, humiliating, empty, while everything that has happened since 1922 is brilliant, glorious, unrivaled elsewhere.

Yet, beneath all the dramatic speeches, beneath the stirring strains of "Giovinezza," persists this horrifying note of discord: *Under Fascism the working masses live, and must live, in material and spiritual poverty.*

To be sure, Italy's economic difficulties in recent years are connected with the general depression in capitalist countries. But recession had begun in Italy already in 1927. Moreover, to point, as many Fascists do, to factors in the world depression as an explanation of the Italian difficulties is not consistent with their claim that Fascism represents a new social and economic order, different from and not subject to the defects of capitalism.

In his leading speech on the Corporative State,[31] Mussolini admitted that Italy was held in the grip of an economic crisis. Yet, "the capitalistic mode of production has been superseded" under Fascism. The Corporative State is developing in Italy an alternative to capitalism and socialism. The corporative system "means regulated economy, and therefore also controlled economy.... The corporations supersede socialism and liberalism; they create a new synthesis. . . . We inherit from both that which was vital in each." The objective of the Corporative State is "to expand the wealth, the political power, and the well-being of the Italian people."

This is the Fascism of the speakers' platform, of the mass

[31] Delivered to the National Council of Corporations, November 14, 1933.

propagandist. But Fascism-in-action is not concerned with fostering the welfare of the working population. Its unique reality is the attempt violently to bolster up the institutions of profit-seeking enterprise by smashing all opposition to the existing order, by ruthessly cutting wages, and by cultivating a servile obedience in the mind of the masses.

Fascism is not an escape from the dilemma of capitalism. Rather, it perpetuates the fundamental contradiction of the system of business enterprise: simultaneous development of the forces of production and restriction of their use for human needs. Armaments and martial activity, maintenance of the parasitic hierarchy of Fascist police and bureaucrats, these are themselves ultimately a staggering burden on profit-seeking enterprise. The inability to function profitably in the impoverished domestic market leads to the ever more desperate necessity of finding external fields for exploitation. This means imperialist adventure and war.

Fascism has not succeeded in so completely suppressing every form of resistance as to permit the unhindered imposition of the discipline of poverty. Among the great masses of workers, peasants, and small proprietors there is grumbling and criticism, resentment against their continually declining incomes, the favors bestowed on big landlords and employers, the high prices charged by the monopolies and the heavy taxes levied by the government, the toll of colonial warfare and the threat of war to come. Such unrest at times breaks forth violently, even in the countryside. Observers report sporadic uprisings against Fascist officials, demonstrations of protest against high taxes, wage cuts, and foreclosure sales, always ending in armed suppression, arrests, and prison sentences.[32]

[32] Seldes, *Sawdust Caesar*, pp. 292-93; Marabini, *Proletariato agricolo*, pp. 106 ff.; Nicoletti, *Le Fascisme contre le paysan*, pp. 95 ff.; *Giustizia e Libertà*, 1934-37, *passim*. Given the press censorship and the general con-

But it cannot be said that this represents an opposition sufficiently organized to constitute an effective threat to Fascism in a moment of crisis.

For it must be recognized that Fascism has been able also to base itself upon popular support. Its emotional appeal and systematic control of the mental life of the nation have not been without effect in diverting the gaze of the masses from "material" to "spiritual values." And the peasants and workers of Italy have always known poverty and hunger. Most serious of all for the Italian people—and for people everywhere—is the intellectual and moral stultification inevitable in such control, and the barriers that it throws in the way of the construction of a more rational society.

---

trols over such information, it is of course possible that these reports are exaggerated. On the other hand, the censorship itself may suppress information on the seriousness of the opposition to Fascism.

Selected Bibliography

I. PUBLICATIONS OF ITALIAN GOVERNMENTAL AND QUASI-GOVERNMENTAL AGENCIES

ARCARI, P. M. I salari agricoli in Italia dal 1905 al 1933. Istituto Centrale di Statistica del Regno d'Italia, Rome, 1934.

CASSA NAZIONALE PER LE ASSICURAZIONI SOCIALI. La disoccupazione e l'assicurazione contro la disoccupazione in Italia, 1919-1924. Rome, 1925.

X COMMISSARIATO PER LE MIGRAZIONI E LA COLONIZZAZIONE INTERNA. Le migrazioni interne, 1934. Rome, 1935.

CONFEDERAZIONE FASCISTA DEL LAVORATORI DELL'AGRICOLTURA. Per le case rurali. Rome, 1934.

——— Problemi corporativi del lavoro agricolo nel campo internazionale. Rome, 1935.

——— Il lavoro agricolo nelle attività delle corporazione. Rome, 1936.

——— L'alimentazione dei lavoratori agricoli in Italia. Rome, 1936.

CONFEDERAZIONE NAZIONALE DEI SINDACATI FASCISTA DELL' AGRICOLTURA. Indagine sulle condizioni di vita dei contadini italiani. Rome, 1930.

——— I salari nell'agricoltura tratti dai contratti di lavoro dal 1913 al 1931. Rome, 1931.

——— L'organizzazione sindacale agricola del Fascismo. Rome, 1932.

CONFEDERAZIONE NAZIONALE FASCISTA DEGLI AGRICOLTORI. Dieci anni di attività sindacale, 1922-1932. Rome, 1933.

FAINA, EUGENIO. Inchiesta parlamentare sulle condizioni dei contadini nelle provincie meridionali e nella Sicilia. 7 vols. Parlamento Italiano, Rome, 1909-11.

FASCIST CONFEDERATION OF INDUSTRIALISTS. ASSOCIATION OF ITALIAN CORPORATIONS. *Business and Financial Report: A*

Monthly Survey of Italian Trade and Industry. Rome, monthly, January 1925-.

X FEDERAZIONE NAZIONALE DELLE BONIFICHE. Le bonifiche in Italia al 1 luglio 1926. Rome, 1927.

ISTITUTO CENTRALE DI STATISTICA DEL REGNO D'ITALIA. *Annuario Statistico Italiano, 1922-25, 1927-37.* 12 vols. Rome, 1926-37.

——— *Bollettino Mensile di Statistica.* Rome, monthly, November 1926-.

——— *Bollettino dei Prezzi.* Rome, monthly, July 1927-.

——— *Bollettino Mensile di Statistica Agraria e Forestale.* Rome, monthly, January 1928-.

——— Censimento della popolazione del Regno d'Italia, 1 dicembre 1921. Vol. XIX: Regno. Rome, 1928.

——— Indagine sulle abitazioni al 21 aprile 1931—IX. Parte II: Tavole. Florence, 1931.

——— Censimento generale dell'bestiame al 19 marzo 1930—VIII. Risultati sommari. Rome, 1933.

——— Censimento delle bonifiche idrauliche di 1ª categorie al 19 marzo 1930—VIII. Rome, 1933.

——— Censimento generale della popolazione del Regno al 21 aprile 1931—IX. Vol. IV: Relazione generale. Parte II: Tavole. Rome, 1934.

——— Indagine sulle case rurali in Italia. Rome, 1934.

——— Catasto agrario 1929. Commento ai primi risultati del nuovo catasto agrario. Rome, 1934.

——— Indici dei prezzi dei prodotti venduti e dei prodotti acquistati dagli agricoltori. Rome, 1935.

——— Censimento generale dell'agricoltura italiana al 19 marzo—VIII. Censimento delle aziende agricole. Rome, 1935.

MINISTERO DEI LAVORI PUBBLICI. Le bonifiche italiane. Rome, 1925.

——— Le opere pubbliche al 30 giugno 1926. Rome, 1927.

MINISTERO DELL'AGRICOLTURA E DELLE FORESTE. I progressi dell'agricoltura italiana in regime fascista. Rome, 1934.

MINISTERO DELLE CORPORAZIONI. *Bollettino del Lavoro e della Previdenza Sociale.* Rome, monthly, October 1929-December 1932.

——— *Sindacato e Corporazione.* Rome, monthly, January 1933-.

MINISTERO DELL'ECONOMIA NAZIONALE. *Bollettino del Lavoro e della Previdenza Sociale.* Rome, monthly, July 1923-September 1929.

——— Il Fascismo e l'agricoltura. Rome, 1929.

MINISTERO DELLE FINANZE. Documenti sulla condizione finanziaria ed economica dell'Italia. Rome, 1923.

——— Il bilancio dello Stato dal 1913-1914 al 1929-1930. Rome, 1931.

MINISTERO DI AGRICOLTURA, INDUSTRIA E COMMERCIO. Censimento generale del bestiame del 19 marzo 1908. Rome, 1910.

MINISTERO PER IL LAVORO. I concordati collettivi di lavoro stipulati dalla Federazione Nazionale dei Lavoratori della Terra nel 1920. Supplement to *Bollettino del Lavoro . . .* No. 36. Rome, 1921.

MINISTERO PER L'AGRICOLTURA. Censimento generale del bestiame nel 1918. Rome, 1921.

MINISTRY OF AGRICULTURE AND FORESTS. The Wheat Campaign in Italy. Rome, 1931.

MINISTRY OF CORPORATIONS. *News Notes on Fascist Corporations.* Rome, monthly, January 1929-.

PARLAMENTO ITALIANO. Atti. Camera dei Deputati. XXVIII Legislatura. Discussioni, 28 novembre 1929-9 aprile 1930. Rome, 1930.

——— Atti. Camera dei Deputati. XXIX Legislatura. Sessione 1934-1935. Rome, 1935.

SERPIERI, ARRIGO. La legge sulla bonifica integrale nel primo anno di applicazione; . . . nel secondo anno . . . ; . . . nel terzo anno . . . ; . . . nel quarto anno . . . ; . . . nel quinto anno . . . Ministero dell'Agricoltura e delle Foreste 5 vols. Rome, 1931-35.

II. OTHER BOOKS AND PERIODICAL ARTICLES

Acerbo, Giacomo. Il riordinamento degli usi civici nel Regno. Rome, 1927.

——— La cooperazione agraria in Italia con notizie sommarie per gli altri paesi. Piacenza, 1932.

——— "La politica agraria in Italia," *La Terra,* March 1930.

Affricano, R. "Lo sviluppo delle migrazioni interne e la politica di ruralizzazione," *Rivista di Politica Economica,* March 1935.

Agreste, V. "Il capitale finanziario in Italia," *Lo Stato Operaio,* July, August 1930.

Aguet, James. La terra ai contadini: Il passato, il presente e l'avvenire della proprietà in Italia. Rome, 1919.

Aimi, Alcide. Verso la scomparsa del salariato. Mantua, 1933.

——— Dalla scomparsa del salariato alla corporazione. Mantua, 1934.

Albertario, P. "L'imponibile di mano d'opera nell'economia agraria del Bassopiano Lombardo," *Giornale degli Economisti e Rivista di Statistica,* December 1932.

Angelini, Franco. "L'Organisation syndicale corporative de l'agriculture en Italie," *La Technique Agricole Internationale,* October-December 1934.

Arcari, P. M. "Statistiche salariali e dinamica dei salari agricoli in Italia," *Economia,* August 1934.

Arias, Gino. La questione meridionale. Bologna, 1919.

Associazione fra le Società Italiane per Azione. *Notizie Statistiche.* Rome, biennially, 1900-1936.

Audoly, Léon. La Protection légale des travailleurs agricoles en Italie. Paris, 1913.

Azimonti, Eugenio. Il Mezzogiorno agrario quale è. Bari, 1921.

Bandino, M. "Il problema della montagna," *Riforma Sociale,* January-February, 1934.

Baravelli, G. C. Integral Land Reclamation in Italy. Rome, 1935.

Beals, Carleton. "Absenteeism, Kissed and Crowned," *Freeman,* March 14, 1923.

BELLUZZO, G. Economia fascista. Rome, 1928.

BIAGI, BRUNO. "The Regulation of Collective Employment Relations in Agriculture in Italy," *International Labour Review*, March 1934.

BOTTAZZI, F., A. NICEFORO, and G. QUAGLIARIELLO. Documenti per lo studio della alimentazione della popolazione italiana nell'ultimo cinquantennio. Naples, 1933.

BOURGIN, G. "La Question agraire en Italie," *Revue d'Économie Politique*, 1912, Nos. 2, 3.

BRIZI, ALESSANDRO. Compartecipazione agrarie e contadini partecipanti in Campania e in Lucania. Istituto Nazionale di Economia Agraria, Rome, 1935.

BUCCELLA, M. R. "Lo svolgimento ed il sistema della bonifica integrale," *Giornale degli Economisti e Rivista di Statistica*, August 1929.

BUSSE, W. "Getreidefeldzug und Weizenerzeugung in Italien," *Berichte über Landwirtschaft*, Vol. X, No. 1, 1929.

——— "Das italienische Meliorationswesen," *Berichte über Landwirtschaft*, 74. Sonderheft: 1933.

CAMPESE, E. Il Fascismo contro la disoccupazione. Rome, 1929.

CHINI, A. "Della piccola proprietà contadina famigliare nell' ordinamento corporativo," *Rivista di Politica Economica*, January 1935.

CIASCA, R. Il problema della terra. Milan, 1921.

COLETTI, FRANCESCO. La popolazione rurale in Italia e i suoi caratteri demografici, psicologici e sociali. Piacenza, 1925.

——— Economia rurale e politica rurale in Italia: Raccolta di studi. Piacenza, 1926.

CONSORZIO NAZIONALE PRODUTTORI ZUCCHERO. L'industria dello zucchero in Italia nel decennio 1924-1933. Genoa, 1934.

COSTANZO, GIULIO. "Share-Tenancy in Italy," *International Review of Agricultural Economics*, No. 1, 1924.

——— "The General Scheme of Land Improvement in Italy," *Monthly Bulletin of Agricultural Economics and Sociology*, April 1929.

——— "Agricultural Co-operation in Italy," *Monthly Bulletin of Agricultural Economics and Sociology*, January 1931.

——— "Comprehensive Reclamation and Land Improvement in Italy," *Monthly Bulletin of Agricultural Economics and Sociology*, May 1934.

——— "System of Agricultural Credit in Italy," *Monthly Bulletin of Agricultural Economics and Sociology*, October 1934.

——— "Corporative Organisation in Italy," *Monthly Bulletin of Agricultural Economics and Sociology*, June 1925.

COTTA, F. Agricultural Co-operation in Fascist Italy. London, 1935.

DAVID, A. La Politique agraire de l'Italie: Les Bonifications. Ministère de l'Agriculture, Paris, 1931.

DEAN, V. M. "The Economic Situation in Italy: The Corporative System," Foreign Policy Association, *Foreign Policy Reports*, January 16, 1935.

DE' STEFANI, A. L'azione dello Stato italiano per le opere pubbliche, 1862-1924. Rome, 1925.

DE VITA, A. "Il reddito dell'Italia al 1928 e la sua ripartizione regionale," *Vita Economica Italiana*, Vol. X, No. 2, 1935.

DI CASTELNUOVO, A. (ed.). Agricoltura e agricoltori in regime fascista. Rome, 1935.

DOBBERT, GERHARD (ed.). Die faschistische Wirtschaft. Berlin, 1934.

DUSMET, G. "Spare Time Organisations for Agricultural Workers in Italy," *International Labour Review*, February 1936.

DUTT, R. P. Fascism and Social Revolution. New York, 1935.

EINZIG, PAUL. The Economic Foundations of Fascism. London, 1933.

ELWIN, W. Fascism at Work. London, 1934.

FARINACCI, R. Un periodo aureo del Partito Nazionale Fascista. Foligno, 1927.

FEDERZONI, LUIGI (ed.). I problemi attuali dell'agricoltura italiana. Bologna, 1933.

FINER, HERMAN. Mussolini's Italy. London, 1935.

FOERSTER, R. E. The Italian Emigration of Our Times. Cambridge, Mass., 1924.

FONTANA, A. "Il contratto di mezzadria dinanzi al Parlamento," *Rivista di Politica Economica,* November 1933.

FORTUNATO, GIUSTINO. Il Mezzogiorno e lo Stato italiano. Florence, 1926.

FRANCIOSA, L. "Bilanci e consumi delle famiglie agricole," *Riforma Sociale,* September-October 1934.

GATTAMORTA, G. Battaglie e realizzazione del sindacalismo fascista: La mezzadria. Rome, 1931.

GIRETTI, E. "Il problema della seta in Italia," *Riforma Sociale,* March-April 1932.

——— "Un momento critico per la seta," *Riforma Sociale,* November-December 1932.

GIUSTIZIA E LIBERTÀ. "I braccianti agricoli in Italia ed il sindacalismo fascista," *Quaderni di Giustizia e Libertà,* December 1932.

GORGOLINI, P. Il Fascismo nella vita italiana. Turin, 1923.

HAIDER, CARMEN. Capital and Labor Under Fascism. New York, 1930.

HAZEN, N. W. "Agricultural Credit in Italy," United States Department of Agriculture, *Foreign Crops and Markets,* September 3, 1935.

HOBSON, ASHER. The Agricultural Survey of Europe: Italy. United States Department of Agriculture, Washington, 1925.

——— "The Landless Agricultural Laborer in Italy," *Journal of Land and Public Utility Economics,* October 1925.

——— "The Collective Leasing and Farming of Land in Italy," *Journal of Land and Public Utility Economics,* January 1926.

INTERNATIONAL INSTITUTE OF AGRICULTURE. Annuaire international de législation agricole. Rome, annually, 1911-.

——— Agricultural Credit and Co-operation in Italy. Rome, 1913.

——— International Yearbook of Agricultural Statistics. Rome, annually, 1912-.

——— The World Agricultural Situation, 1933-1934. Rome, 1935.

INTERNATIONAL LABOUR OFFICE. "Collective Labour Agreements in Italian Agriculture," *International Labour Review*, November 1926, January 1927.

——— Collective Agreements in Agriculture. Geneva, 1933.

——— "Regulation of Collective Employment Relations in Agriculture in Italy," *International Labour Review*, March 1934.

——— "Statistics of Wages of Agricultural Workers in Various Countries, 1927-1934," *International Labour Review*, November-December 1934.

ISTITUTO NAZIONALE DI ECONOMIA AGRARIA. Monografie di famiglie rurali. 11 vols. Rome, 1931-35.

——— Inchiesta sulla piccola proprietà coltivatrice formatasi nel dopoguerra. Rome, 1931-35.

JACINI, STEFANO. Atti della Giunta per la Inchiesta Agraria: Relazione finale. Rome, 1885.

——— L'Inchiesta Agraria. Piacenza, 1926.

JANDOLO, E. Le leggi per la bonifica integrale. Padua, 1926.

——— "I precedenti della nuova legge sulla bonifica integrale," *L'Italia Agricolo*, October, November 1932.

LENTI, L. "L'industria zootecnica italiana: Prospettive d'incrementi e di miglioramenti," *Annali di Economia*, Vol. VI, 1930.

LEONHARD, R. Die landwirtschaftlichen Zustände in Italien. Hanover, 1915.

LIEBE, H. "Italiens Gartenbau," *Berichte über Landwirtschaft*, 103. Sonderheft: 1935.

LLOYD, E. A. The Co-operative Movement in Italy. London, 1925.

LONGOBARDI, CESARE. Land Reclamation in Italy. London, 1936.

LORENZONI, G. "Latifundia in Sicily and Their Possible Transformation," International Institute of Agriculture, *International Review of Agriculture*, No. 3, 1923.

——— "Recent Agrarian Policy in Italy and the Problem of

Latifundia," International Institute of Agriculture, *International Review of Agricultural Economics*, January-March 1925.

McGuire, C. E. Italy's International Economic Position. New York, 1927.

Mannhardt, J. W. Der Faschismus. Munich, 1925.

Marabini, A. "Le tasse e i contadini," *Lo Stato Operaio*, December 1934.

——— Proletariato agricolo e fascismo in Italia. Brussels, 1935.

——— "La mezzadria in Italia," *Lo Stato Operaio*, March 1936.

Masé, D. "Distribuzione del reddito nell'agricoltura italiana," *Rivista di Politica Economica*, July-August 1931.

Mazzocchi-Alemanni, N. "I debiti dell'agricoltura," *Giornale degli Economisti e Rivista di Statistica*, August 1932.

——— "Le case rurali," *Atti della R. Accademia dei Georgofili*, April-June 1934.

Meliadò, L. "Il reddito privato degli italiani nel 1928," *Vita Economica Italiana*, Vol. 6, No. 1, 1931.

Messedaglia, L. Per la storia dell'agricoltura e dell'alimentazione. Piacenza, 1932.

Mitzakis, Michel. Les Grandes problèmes italiens: L'Économie, les finances et les dettes. Paris, 1931.

Mortara, A. Doveri sociali della proprietà fondiaria. Rome, 1913.

Mortara, Giorgio. *Prospettive Economiche.* Castello, annually, 1921-36.

——— "Sulla politica doganale italiana del dopoguerra," *Annali di Economia*, June 1934.

Müller-Einhart, E. Mussolinis Getreideschlacht: Italienische Landwirtschaft im Zeichen der Diktatur. Regensburg, 1933.

Mussolini, Benito. I discorsi della rivoluzione. Milan, 1927.

——— Discorsi del 1925; . . . 1926; . . . 1927; . . . 1928; . . . 1929; . . . 1930. Milan, 1926-31.

——— L'agricoltura e i rurali: Discorsi e scritti. Rome, 1931.

——— Scritti e discorsi dal 1932 al 1933. Milan, 1934.
——— Fascism: Doctrine and Institutions. Rome, 1935.
NANNINI, S. "Le migrazioni e la colonizzazione," *Conquista della Terra,* December 1935.
NEGRI, G. Le Riz en Italie. Milan, 1934.
NICOLAI, A. Les Remises des emigrants italiens. Nice, 1935.
NICOLETTI, M. Le Fascisme contre le paysan: L'Éxperience italienne. Paris, 1929.
OBLATH, A. "The Campaign Against Unemployment in Italy," *International Labour Review,* May 1930.
——— "Italian Emigration and Colonisation Policy," *International Labour Review,* June 1931.
OCCHINI, P. L. La crisi agraria in Italia. Florence, 1921.
PAGANI, A. I braccianti della valle padana. Rome, 1932.
——— Le compartecipazione agricole del Mantovano. Milan, 1933.
PARESCHI, C. "Gli ammassi collettivi di grano e la loro organizzazione," *Cooperazione Rurale,* March 1935.
PERROUX, F. Contribution à l'étude de l'économie et des finances publiques de l'Italie depuis la guerre. Paris, 1929.
PESCE, G. Contadini d'Italia. Bologna, 1926.
PITIGLIANI, FAUSTO. The Italian Corporative State. New York, 1934.
POR, ODON. Guilds and Co-operatives in Italy. London, 1923.
——— Fascism. London, 1923.
PRITZKOLEIT, K. "Der italienische Agrarkredit," *Wirtschaftsdienst,* October 4, 1935.
PUGLIESE, S. "Produzione, salari e redditi in una regione risicola italiana," *Annali di Economia,* January 1927.
R. ACCADEMIA DEI GEORGOFILI. "Convegno per la bonifica integrale, Firenze, 21-22 maggio 1934," *Atti della R. Accademia dei Georgofili,* July-September 1934.
RÉPACI, F. "La misura delle variazione delle tariffe doganale," *Riforma Sociale,* September-October 1934
RIVERA, VINCENZO. Il problema agronomico del Mezzogiorno. Rome, 1924.
——— Battaglie per il grano. Aquila, 1925.

ROBERTI, R. "Lo sviluppo delle assicurazioni sociali in agricoltura," *La Terra*, May 1933.

ROCCA, G. "L'occupazione delle terre 'incolte,'" *Riforma Sociale*, May-June 1920.

ROCQUIGNY DU FAYEL, H. M. R. DE. Le Prolétariat rural en Italie: Ligues et grèves de paysans. Paris, 1904.

ROSENSTOCK-FRANCK, L. L'Économie corporative fasciste en doctrine et en fait. Paris, 1934.

ROTA, F. "La crisi e l'agricoltura italiana," *L'Assistenza Sociale Agricola*, April-May 1933.

ROUX, PAUL. La Question agraire en Italie: Le Latifundium romain. Paris, 1910.

ROYAL INSTITUTE OF ECONOMIC AFFAIRS. The Economic and Financial Position of Italy. London, 1935.

RUINI, M. "The Co-operative Movement in Italy," *International Labour Review*, January 1922.

SALVEMINI, GAETANO. The Fascist Dictatorship in Italy. New York, 1927.

——— "Mussolini's Battle of Wheat," *Political Science Quarterly*, March 1931.

——— "Land Reclamation and Fascism," *Italy Today*, May-June 1932.

——— "Italian Unemployment Statistics," *Social Research*, August 1934.

——— "Twelve Years of Fascist Finance," *Foreign Affairs*, April 1935.

——— "Can Italy Live at Home?" *Foreign Affairs*, January 1936.

——— "Economic Forces in Italy," *Yale Review*, Spring 1936.

——— Under the Axe of Fascism. New York, 1936.

SARTORIUS VON WALTERSHAUSEN, AUGUST. Die sizilianische Agrarverfassung und ihre Wandlungen, 1780-1912. Leipzig, 1913.

SCHNEIDER, H. W. Making the Fascist State. New York, 1928.

SCHNEIDER, H. W., and S. B. CLOUGH. Making Fascists. Chicago, 1929.

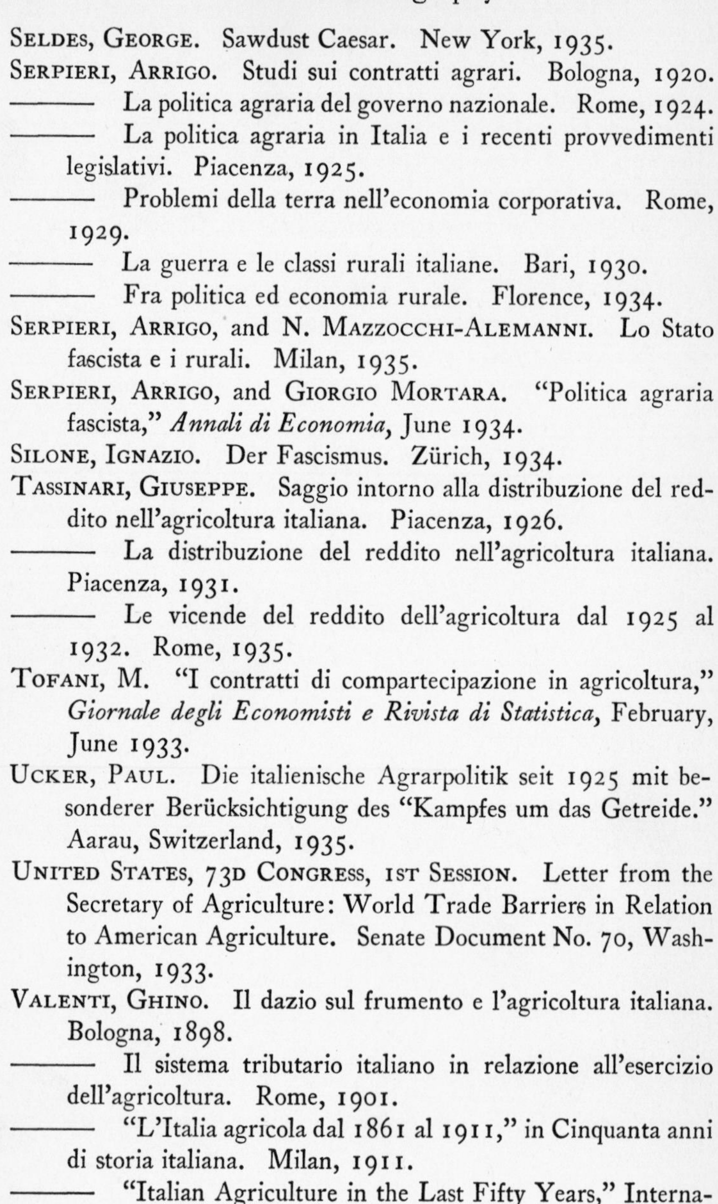

Seldes, George. Sawdust Caesar. New York, 1935.

Serpieri, Arrigo. Studi sui contratti agrari. Bologna, 1920.

——— La politica agraria del governo nazionale. Rome, 1924.

——— La politica agraria in Italia e i recenti provvedimenti legislativi. Piacenza, 1925.

——— Problemi della terra nell'economia corporativa. Rome, 1929.

——— La guerra e le classi rurali italiane. Bari, 1930.

——— Fra politica ed economia rurale. Florence, 1934.

Serpieri, Arrigo, and N. Mazzocchi-Alemanni. Lo Stato fascista e i rurali. Milan, 1935.

Serpieri, Arrigo, and Giorgio Mortara. "Politica agraria fascista," *Annali di Economia*, June 1934.

Silone, Ignazio. Der Fascismus. Zürich, 1934.

Tassinari, Giuseppe. Saggio intorno alla distribuzione del reddito nell'agricoltura italiana. Piacenza, 1926.

——— La distribuzione del reddito nell'agricoltura italiana. Piacenza, 1931.

——— Le vicende del reddito dell'agricoltura dal 1925 al 1932. Rome, 1935.

Tofani, M. "I contratti di compartecipazione in agricoltura," *Giornale degli Economisti e Rivista di Statistica*, February, June 1933.

Ucker, Paul. Die italienische Agrarpolitik seit 1925 mit besonderer Berücksichtigung des "Kampfes um das Getreide." Aarau, Switzerland, 1935.

United States, 73d Congress, 1st Session. Letter from the Secretary of Agriculture: World Trade Barriers in Relation to American Agriculture. Senate Document No. 70, Washington, 1933.

Valenti, Ghino. Il dazio sul frumento e l'agricoltura italiana. Bologna, 1898.

——— Il sistema tributario italiano in relazione all'esercizio dell'agricoltura. Rome, 1901.

——— "L'Italia agricola dal 1861 al 1911," in Cinquanta anni di storia italiana. Milan, 1911.

——— "Italian Agriculture in the Last Fifty Years," International Institute of Agriculture, *Bulletin of the Bureau of Economic and Social Intelligence,* August, September 1912.

Vandelli, G. "La marcia della concentrazione industriale," *Lo Stato Operaio,* July 1928.

Virgilii, F. L'Italia agricola odierna. Milan, 1930.

Vöchting, Friedrich. Die Romagna: Eine Studie über Halbpacht und Landarbeiterwesen in Italien. Karlsruhe, 1927.

——— "Die italienische Getreideschlacht," *Schmollers Jahrbuch,* Vol. LIV, No. 5, 1930.

——— "Die faschistische Agrarpolitik," *Wirtschaftsring,* March 9, 1934.

——— Die Urbarmachung der römischen Campagna. Zürich, 1935.

Volpe, G. Lo sviluppo storico del Fascismo. Palermo, 1928.

——— "Fascismo: Storia," in Enciclopedia Italiana, Vol. XIV.

Walter, Karl. Co-operation in Changing Italy: A Survey. London, 1934.

Index

valetudinarian